THE PLACES THAT SCARE YOU

The Places That Scare You

A GUIDE TO FEARLESSNESS
IN DIFFICULT TIMES

PEMA CHÖDRÖN

SHAMBHALA
Boston
2007

Shambhala Publications, Inc.
Horticultural Hall
300 Massachusetts Avenue
Boston, Massachusetts 02115
www.shambhala.com

© 2001 by Pema Chödrön

Epigraph on page 116 from "Timely Rain" by Chögyam Trungpa. From *Timely Rain* by Chögyam Trungpa. © 1972, 1983, 1998 by Diana J. Mukpo. Reprinted by arrangement with Shambhala Publications, Inc., Boston, MA, 02115.

Four Limitless Ones chant as presented in appendix 2 is translated by the Nālandā Translation Committee.

Translation of *The Root Text of the Seven Points of Training the Mind* © 1981, 1986 by Chögyam Trungpa; revised translation © 1993 by Diana J. Mukpo and the Nālandā Translation Committee. All rights reserved.

The author's proceeds from this book will be donated to Gampo Abbey, Pleasant Bay, Nova Scotia, Canada B0E 2P0.

Cover photograph by Michael Wood

9 8 7 6 5

PRINTED IN THE UNITED STATES OF AMERICA

Distributed in the United States by Random House, Inc.,
and in Canada by Random House of Canada Ltd

ISBN 978-1-59030-449-5

To the Sixteenth Karmapa,
Rangjung Rigpe Dorje,
Dilgo Khyentse Rinpoche,
and Chögyam Trungpa Rinpoche,
who taught me what it means
to be fearless.

Confess your hidden faults.
Approach what you find repulsive.
Help those you think you cannot help.
Anything you are attached to, let it go.
Go to places that scare you.

—ADVICE FROM HER TEACHER
TO THE TIBETAN YOGINI
MACHIK LABDRÖN

CONTENTS

CONTENTS

ACKNOWLEDGMENTS

THERE ARE FIVE PEOPLE whom I particularly want to thank for helping bring this book to life: my monastic brother Tingdzin Ötro, whose work on my talks was invaluable; Tamar Ellentuck, who was an excellent and loyal secretary to me through some very difficult times; Gigi Sims, transcriber extraordinaire; my good friend Helen Tworkov, who gave me the perfect place to write; and most of all, my longtime friend and editor, Emily Hilburn Sell, who put her whole heart into this book, extending herself with fearless warriorship.

I would also like to thank the many other people who have transcribed my talks over the past five years: Migme Chödrön, Lynne Van de Bunte, Eugene and Helen Tashima, Susan Stowens, Alexis Shaw, Bill and Eileen Fell, Rohana Greenwood, and Barbara Blouin.

I wish to thank Soledad González for her loving-kindness.

My profound appreciation goes to Jōko Beck and Ezra Bayda, whose work has had a major influence on me. In particular I want to acknowledge Ezra's influence in the chapter on meditation.

ACKNOWLEDGMENTS ·

Finally, I express my heartfelt gratitude to my living teachers, Dzigar Kongtrul Rinpoche and Sakyong Mipham Rinpoche. They are generous enough to continually show me the nature of my mind and reveal my hidden faults.

THE PLACES THAT SCARE YOU

Prologue

W HEN I TEACH, I begin with a compassionate aspiration. I express the wish that we will apply the teachings in our everyday lives and thus free ourselves and others from suffering.

During the talk, I encourage the audience to keep an open mind. This is often likened to the wonder of a child seeing the world without preconceptions. As the Zen master Suzuki Roshi put it, "In the beginner's mind there are many possibilities, but in the expert's there are few."

At the end of the talk, I dedicate the merit of the occasion to all beings. This gesture of universal friendship has been likened to a drop of fresh springwater. If we put it on a rock in the sunshine, it will soon evaporate. If we put it in the ocean, however, it will never be lost. Thus the wish is made that we not keep the teachings to ourselves but use them to benefit others.

This approach reflects what are called the three noble principles: good in the beginning, good in the middle, good at the end. They can be used in all the activities of our lives. We can begin anything we do—start our day, eat a meal, or walk into a meeting—with the intention to be open, flexible, and kind. Then we can proceed with an inquisitive attitude. As my teacher Chögyam Trungpa Rinpoche used to say, "Live your life as an experiment."

At the end of the activity, whether we feel we have succeeded or failed in our intention, we seal the act by thinking of others, of those who are succeeding and failing all over the world. We wish that anything we learned in our experiment could also benefit them.

In this spirit, I offer this guide on the training of the compassionate warrior. May it be of benefit at the beginning, in the middle, and at the end. May it help move us toward the places that scare us. May it inform our lives and help us to die with no regrets.

1

The Excellence of Bodhichitta

> It is only with the heart that one can see rightly;
> what is essential is invisible to the eye.
>
> —ANTOINE DE SAINT-EXUPÉRY

WHEN I WAS ABOUT SIX YEARS OLD I received the essential bodhichitta teaching from an old woman sitting in the sun. I was walking by her house one day feeling lonely, unloved, and mad, kicking anything I could find. Laughing, she said to me, "Little girl, don't you go letting life harden your heart."

Right there, I received this pith instruction: we can let the circumstances of our lives harden us so that we become increasingly resentful and afraid, or we can let them soften us and make us kinder and more open to what scares us. We always have this choice.

If we were to ask the Buddha, "What is bodhichitta?" he might tell us that this word is easier to understand than to translate. He might encourage us to seek out ways to find its meaning in our own lives. He might tantalize us by adding that it is only bodhichitta that heals, that bodhichitta is capable of transforming the hardest of hearts and the most prejudiced and fearful of minds.

Chitta means "mind" and also "heart" or "attitude." *Bodhi* means "awake," "enlightened," or "completely open." Sometimes the completely open heart and mind of bodhichitta is called the soft spot, a place as vulnerable and tender as an open wound. It is equated, in part, with our ability to love. Even the cruelest people have this soft spot. Even the most vicious animals love their offspring. As Trungpa Rinpoche put it, "Everybody loves something, even if it's only tortillas."

Bodhichitta is also equated, in part, with compassion—our ability to feel the pain that we share with others. Without realizing it we continually shield ourselves from this pain because it scares us. We put up protective walls made of opinions, prejudices, and strategies, barriers that are built on a deep fear of being hurt. These walls are further fortified by emotions of all kinds: anger, craving, indifference, jealousy and envy, arrogance and pride. But fortunately for us, the soft spot—our innate ability to love and to care about things—is like a crack in these walls we erect. It's a natural opening in the barriers we create when we're afraid. With practice we can learn to find this opening. We can learn to seize that vulnerable moment—love, gratitude, loneliness, embarrassment, inadequacy—to awaken bodhichitta.

An analogy for bodhichitta is the rawness of a broken heart. Sometimes this broken heart gives birth to anxiety and panic, sometimes to anger, resentment, and blame. But under the hardness of that armor there is the tenderness of genuine sadness. This is our link with all those who have ever loved. This genuine heart of sadness can teach us great compassion. It can humble us when we're arrogant and soften us when we are unkind. It awakens us when we prefer to sleep and pierces through our indifference. This continual ache of the heart is a blessing that when accepted fully can be shared with all.

The Buddha said that we are never separated from enlightenment. Even at the times we feel most stuck, we are never alienated from the awakened state. This is a revolutionary assertion. Even ordinary people like us with hang-ups and confusion have this mind of enlightenment called bodhichitta. The openness and warmth of bodhichitta is in fact our true nature and condition. Even when our neurosis feels far more basic than our wisdom, even when we're feeling most confused and hopeless, bodhichitta—like the open sky—is always here, undiminished by the clouds that temporarily cover it.

Given that we are so familiar with the clouds, of course, we may find the Buddha's teaching hard to believe. Yet the truth is that in the midst of our suffering, in the hardest of times, we can contact this noble heart of bodhichitta. It is always available, in pain as well as in joy.

A young woman wrote to me about finding herself in a small town in the Middle East surrounded by people jeering, yelling, and threatening to throw stones at her and her friends because they were Americans. Of course, she was terrified, and what happened to her is interesting. Suddenly she identified with every person throughout history who had ever been scorned and hated. She understood what it was like to be despised for any reason: ethnic group, racial background, sexual preference, gender. Something cracked wide open and she stood in the shoes of millions of oppressed people and saw with a new perspective. She even understood her shared humanity with those who hated her. This sense of deep connection, of belonging to the same family, is bodhichitta.

Bodhichitta exists on two levels. First there is unconditional bodhichitta, an immediate experience that is refreshingly free of concept, opinion, and our usual all-caught-upness. It's something hugely good that we are not able to pin down even slightly, like knowing at gut level that there's absolutely nothing to lose. Second there is relative bodhichitta, our ability to keep our hearts and minds open to suffering without shutting down.

Those who train wholeheartedly in awakening

unconditional and relative bodhichitta are called bodhisattvas or warriors—not warriors who kill and harm but warriors of nonaggression who hear the cries of the world. These are men and women who are willing to train in the middle of the fire. Training in the middle of the fire can mean that warrior-bodhisattvas enter challenging situations in order to alleviate suffering. It also refers to their willingness to cut through personal reactivity and self-deception, to their dedication to uncovering the basic undistorted energy of bodhichitta. We have many examples of master warriors—people like Mother Teresa and Martin Luther King Jr.—who recognized that the greatest harm comes from our own aggressive minds. They devoted their lives to helping others understand this truth. There are also many ordinary people who spend their lives training in opening their hearts and minds in order to help others do the same. Like them, we could learn to relate to ourselves and our world as warriors. We could train in awakening our courage and love.

There are both formal and informal methods for helping us to cultivate this bravery and kindness. There are practices for nurturing our capacity to rejoice, to let go, to love, and to shed a tear. There are those that teach us to stay open to uncertainty. There are others that help us to stay present at the times that we habitually shut down.

Wherever we are, we can train as a warrior. The practices of meditation, loving-kindness, compassion, joy, and equanimity are our tools. With the help of these practices, we can uncover the soft spot of bodhichitta. We will find that tenderness in sorrow and in gratitude. We will find it behind the hardness of rage and in the shakiness of fear. It is available in loneliness as well as in kindness.

Many of us prefer practices that will not cause discomfort, yet at the same time we want to be healed. But bodhichitta training doesn't work that way. A warrior accepts that we can never know what will happen to us next. We can try to control the uncontrollable by looking for security and predictability, always hoping to be comfortable and safe. But the truth is that we can never avoid uncertainty. This not knowing is part of the adventure, and it's also what makes us afraid.

Bodhichitta training offers no promise of happy endings. Rather, this "I" who wants to find security—who wants something to hold on to—can finally learn to grow up. The central question of a warrior's training is not how we avoid uncertainty and fear but how we relate to discomfort. How do we practice with difficulty, with our emotions, with the unpredictable encounters of an ordinary day?

All too frequently we relate like timid birds who don't dare to leave the nest. Here we sit in a nest that's getting pretty smelly and that hasn't served its function for a very long time. No one is arriving to feed us. No one is protecting us and keeping us warm. And yet we keep hoping mother bird will arrive.

We could do ourselves the ultimate favor and finally get out of that nest. That this takes courage is obvious. That we could use some helpful hints is also clear. We may doubt that we're up to being a warrior-in-training. But we can ask ourselves this question: "Do I prefer to grow up and relate to life directly, or do I choose to live and die in fear?"

All beings have the capacity to feel tenderness—to experience heartbreak, pain, and uncertainty. Therefore the enlightened heart of bodhichitta is available to us all. The insight meditation teacher Jack Kornfield tells of witnessing this in Cambodia during the time of the Khmer Rouge. Fifty thousand people had become communists at gunpoint, threatened with death if they continued their Buddhist practices. In spite of the danger, a temple was established in the refugee camp, and twenty thousand people attended the opening ceremony. There were no lectures or prayers but simply continuous chanting of one of the central teachings of the Buddha:

> Hatred never ceases by hatred
> But by love alone is healed.
> This is an ancient and eternal law.

Thousands of people chanted and wept, knowing that the truth in these words was even greater than their suffering.

Bodhichitta has this kind of power. It will inspire and support us in good times and bad. It is like discovering a wisdom and courage we do not even know we have. Just as alchemy changes any metal into gold, bodhichitta can, if we let it, transform any activity, word, or thought into a vehicle for awakening our compassion.

2

Tapping Into the Spring

A human being is a part of the whole called
by us "the universe," a part limited in time
and space. He experiences himself, his
thoughts and feelings, as something separate
from the rest—a kind of optical delusion of
consciousness. This delusion is a kind of prison
for us, restricting us to our personal desires and
affection for a few persons nearest to us. Our task
must be to free ourselves from this prison by
widening the circle of understanding and
compassion to embrace all living creatures
and the whole of nature in its beauty.

—ALBERT EINSTEIN

WHEN WE WERE DIGGING the foundation for
the retreat center at Gampo Abbey, we hit
bedrock, and a small crack appeared. A minute later
water was dripping out. An hour later, the flow was
stronger and the crack was wider.

Finding the basic goodness of bodhichitta is like
that—tapping into a spring of living water that has

been temporarily encased in solid rock. When we touch the center of sorrow, when we sit with discomfort without trying to fix it, when we stay present to the pain of disapproval or betrayal and let it soften us, these are the times that we connect with bodhichitta.

Tapping into that shaky and tender place has a transformative effect. Being in this place may feel uncertain and edgy but it's also a big relief. Just to stay there, even for a moment, feels like a genuine act of kindness to ourselves. Being compassionate enough to accommodate our own fears takes courage, of course, and it definitely feels counterintuitive. But it's what we need to do.

It's hard to know whether to laugh or to cry at the human predicament. Here we are with so much wisdom and tenderness, and—without even knowing it—we cover it over to protect ourselves from insecurity. Although we have the potential to experience the freedom of a butterfly, we mysteriously prefer the small and fearful cocoon of ego.

A friend was telling me about her elderly parents in Florida. They live in an area where there's poverty and hardship; the threat of violence seems very real. Their way of relating to this is to live in a walled community protected by guard dogs and electric gates. It is their hope, of course, that nothing scary will enter. Unfortunately, my friend's parents are becoming more and more afraid to go outside those walls. They want to go to the beach or the golf course, but they're too scared to budge. Even though they now pay someone to do their shopping, the feeling of insecurity is getting stronger. Lately they've become paranoid even about those who are allowed through the gates: the people who fix broken appliances, the gardeners, the plumbers, and the electricians. Through their isolation, they are becoming unable to cope with an unpredictable world. This is an accurate analogy for the workings of ego.

As Albert Einstein pointed out, the tragedy of experiencing ourselves as apart from everyone else is that this delusion becomes a prison. Sadder yet, we become increasingly unnerved at the possibility of freedom. When the barriers come down, we don't know what to do. We need a bit more warning about what it feels like when the walls start tumbling down. We need to be told that fear and trembling accompany growing up and that letting go takes courage. Finding the courage to go to the places that scare us cannot happen without compassionate inquiry into the workings of ego. So we ask ourselves, "What do I do when I feel I can't handle what's going on? Where do I look for strength and in what do I place my trust?"

The Buddha taught that flexibility and openness bring strength and that running from groundlessness weakens us and brings pain. But do we understand that becoming familiar with the running away is the key? Openness doesn't come from resisting our fears but from getting to know them well.

Rather than going after those walls and barriers with a sledgehammer, we pay attention to them. With gentleness and honesty, we move closer to those walls. We touch them and smell them and get to know them well. We begin a process of acknowledging our aversions and our cravings. We become familiar with the strategies and beliefs we use to build the walls: What are the stories I tell myself? What repels me and what attracts me? We start to get curious about what's going on. Without calling what we see right or wrong, we simply look as objectively as we can. We can observe ourselves with humor, not getting overly serious, moralistic, or uptight about this investigation. Year after year, we train in remaining open and receptive to whatever arises. Slowly, very slowly, the cracks in the walls seem to widen and, as if by magic, bodhichitta is able to flow freely.

A teaching that supports us in this process of unblocking bodhichitta is that of the three lords of materialism. These are the three ways that we shield ourselves from this fluid, un-pin-downable world, three strategies we use to provide ourselves with the illusion of security. This teaching encourages us to become very familiar with these strategies of ego, to see clearly how we continue to seek comfort and ease in ways that only strengthen our fears.

The first of the three lords of materialism is called the lord of form. It represents how we look to externals to give us solid ground. We can begin to pay attention to our methods of escape. What do I do when I feel anxious and depressed, bored or lonely? Is "shopping therapy" my way of coping? Or do I turn to alcohol or food? Do I cheer myself up with drugs or sex, or do I seek adventure? Do I prefer retreating into the beauty of nature or into the delicious world provided by a really good book? Do I fill up the space by making phone calls, by surfing the net, by watching hours of TV? Some of these methods are dangerous, some are humorous, some are quite benign. The point is that we can misuse any substance or activity to run away from insecurity. When we become addicted to the lord of form, we are creating the causes and conditions for suffering to escalate. We can't get any lasting satisfaction no matter how hard we try. Instead the very feelings we're trying to escape from get stronger.

A traditional analogy for the pain caused by the lord of form is of a mouse being caught in a trap because it can't resist eating the cheese. The Dalai Lama offers an interesting twist on this analogy. He says that when he was a boy in Tibet he used to try to catch the mice, not because he wished to kill them, but because he wanted to outsmart them. He says that the mice in Tibet must be more clever than ordinary mice because he never succeeded in catching one. Instead they became his models of enlightened conduct. He felt that, unlike most of us, they had figured out that the best thing they could do for themselves was to refrain from the short-term pleasure of cheese in order to have the long-term pleasure of living. He encouraged us to follow their example.

No matter how we get trapped, our usual reaction is not to become curious about what's happening. We do not naturally investigate the strategies of ego. Most of us just blindly reach for something familiar that we associate with relief and then wonder why we stay dissatisfied. The radical approach of bodhichitta practice is to pay attention to what we do. Without judging it we train in kindly acknowledging whatever is going on. Eventually we might decide to stop hurting ourselves in the same old ways.

The second of the three lords of materialism is the lord of speech. This lord represents how we use beliefs of all kinds to give us the illusion of certainty about the nature of reality. Any of the "isms"—political, ecological, philosophical, or spiritual—can be misused in this way. "Political correctness" is a good example of how this lord operates. When we believe in the correctness of our view, we can be very narrow-minded and prejudiced about the faults of other people.

For example, how do I react when my beliefs about the government are challenged? How about when others don't agree with how I feel about homosexuality or women's rights or the environment? What happens when my ideas about smoking or drinking are challenged? What do I do when my religious convictions are not shared?

New practitioners often embrace meditation or the

Buddhist teachings with passionate enthusiasm. We feel part of a new group, glad to have a new perspective. But do we then judge people who see the world differently? Do we close our minds to others because they don't believe in karma?

The problem isn't with the beliefs themselves but with how we use them to get ground under our feet, how we use them to feel right and to make someone else wrong, how we use them to avoid feeling the uneasiness of not knowing what is going on. It reminds me of a fellow I knew in the 1960s whose passion was for protesting against injustice. Whenever it looked as if a conflict would be resolved, he would sink into a kind of gloom. When a new cause for outrage arose, he'd become elated again.

Jarvis Jay Masters is a Buddhist friend of mine living on death row. In his book, *Finding Freedom*, he tells a story about what happens when we are seduced by the lord of speech.

One night he was sitting on his bed reading when his neighbor, Omar, yelled out, "Hey, Jarvis, check out channel seven." Jarvis had the picture on without the sound. He looked up and saw a lot of enraged people waving their arms in the air. He said, "Hey, Omar, what's going on?" and his neighbor told him, "It's the Ku Klux Klan, Jarvis, and they're yelling and screaming about how everything's the fault of the blacks and the Jews."

A few minutes later, Omar hollered, "Hey, check out

what's happening now." Jarvis looked up at his television and he saw a large group of people marching, waving placards, and getting arrested. He said, "I can see just by looking at them that they're really angry about something. What's up with all those people?" Omar said, "Jarvis, that's an environmentalists' demonstration. They're demanding an end to cutting down trees and killing seals and everything. See that one woman raging into the microphone and all those people screaming?"

Ten minutes later Omar called out again, "Hey, Jarvis! Are you still watching? Can you see what's happening now?" Jarvis looked up and this time he saw a lot of people in suits looking like they were in a real uproar about something. He said, "What's up with these guys?" and Omar answered, "Jarvis, that's the president and the senators of the United States and they're fighting and arguing right there on national TV, each trying to convince the public that the other is at fault for this terrible economy."

Jarvis said, "Well, Omar, I sure learned something interesting tonight. Whether they're wearing Klan outfits or environmentalist outfits or really expensive suits, all these people have the same angry faces."

Being caught by the lord of speech may start with just a reasonable conviction about what we feel to be true. However, if we find ourselves becoming righteously indignant, that's a sure sign that we've gone too far and that our ability to effect change will be hindered. Beliefs and ideals have become just another way to put up walls.

The third lord, the lord of mind, uses the most subtle and seductive strategy of all. The lord of mind comes into play when we attempt to avoid uneasiness by seeking special states of mind. We can use drugs this way. We can use sports. We can use falling in love. We can use spiritual practices. There are many ways to obtain altered states of mind. These special states are addictive. It feels so good to break free from our mundane experience. We want more. For example, new meditators often expect that with training they can transcend the pain of ordinary life. It's disappointing, to say the least, to be told to touch down into the thick of things, to remain open and receptive to boredom as well as bliss.

Sometimes, out of the blue, people have amazing experiences. Recently a lawyer told me that while standing on a street corner waiting for the light to change an extraordinary thing occurred. Suddenly her body expanded until it felt as big as the entire universe. She felt instinctively that she and the universe were one. She had no doubt that this was actually true. She knew she was not, as she'd previously assumed, separate from everything else.

Needless to say, the experience shook up her beliefs and made her question what we do with our lives, spending so much time trying to protect the illusion of our personal territory. She understood how this predicament leads to the wars and violence that are escalating all over the globe. The problem arose when she started hanging on to her experience, when she wanted it back. Ordinary perception was no longer satisfying: it left her feeling troubled and out of touch. She felt that if she couldn't stay in that altered state she'd just as soon be dead.

In the sixties I knew people who took LSD every day with the belief that they could maintain that high. Instead they fried their brains. I still know men and women who are addicted to falling in love. Like Don Juan, they can't bear it when that initial glow begins to wear off; they're always seeking out someone new.

Even though peak experiences might show us the truth and inform us about why we are training, they are essentially no big deal. If we can't integrate them into the ups and downs of our lives, if we cling to them, they will hinder us. We can trust our experiences as valid, but then we have to move on and learn to get along with our neighbors. Then even the most remarkable insights can begin to permeate our lives. As the twelfth-century Tibetan yogi Milarepa said when he heard of his student Gampopa's peak experiences, "They are neither good nor bad. Keep meditating." It isn't the special states themselves that are the problem, it's their addictive quality. Since it is inevitable that what goes up must come down, when we take refuge in the lord of mind we are doomed to disappointment.

Each of us has a variety of habitual tactics for avoiding life as it is. In a nutshell, that's the message of the three lords of materialism. This simple teaching is, it seems, everyone's autobiography. When we use these strategies we become less able to enjoy the tenderness and wonder that is available in the most unremarkable of times. Connecting with bodhichitta is ordinary.

When we don't run from everyday uncertainty, we can contact bodhichitta. It's a natural force that wants to emerge. It is, in fact, unstoppable. Once we stop blocking it with ego's strategies, the refreshing water of bodhichitta will definitely begin to flow. We can slow it down. We can dam it up. Nevertheless, whenever there's an opening, bodhichitta will always appear, like those weeds and flowers that pop out of the sidewalk as soon as there's a crack.

3

The Facts of Life

> A fresh attitude starts to happen when we look
> to see that yesterday was yesterday, and now it is
> gone; today is today and now it is new. It is like
> that—every hour, every minute is changing. If
> we stop observing change, then we stop seeing
> everything as new.
>
> —DZIGAR KONGTRUL RINPOCHE

THE BUDDHA TAUGHT that there are three principal characteristics of human existence: impermanence, egolessness, and suffering or dissatisfaction. According to the Buddha, the lives of all beings are marked by these three qualities. Recognizing these qualities to be real and true in our own experience helps us to relax with things as they are.

When I first heard this teaching it seemed academic and remote. But when I was encouraged to pay attention—to be curious about what was happening with my body and my mind—something shifted. I could observe from my own experience that nothing is static. My moods are continuously shifting like the weather. I am definitely not in control of what thoughts or emotions are going to arise, nor can I halt their flow. Stillness is followed by movement, movement flows back into stillness. Even the most persistent physical pain, when I pay attention to it, changes like the tides.

I feel gratitude to the Buddha for pointing out that what we struggle against all our lives can be acknowledged as ordinary experience. Life *does* continually go up and down. People and situations *are* unpredictable, and so is everything else. Everybody knows the pain of getting what we don't want: saints, sinners, winners, losers. I feel gratitude that someone saw the truth and pointed out that we don't suffer this kind of pain because of our personal inability to get things right.

That nothing is static or fixed, that all is fleeting and impermanent, is the first mark of existence. It is the ordinary state of affairs. Everything is in process. Everything—every tree, every blade of grass, all the animals, insects, human beings, buildings, the animate and the inanimate—is always changing, moment to moment. We don't have to be mystics or physicists to know this. Yet at the level of personal experience, we resist this basic fact. It means that life isn't always going to go our way. It means there's loss as well as gain. And we don't like that.

Once I was changing jobs and houses at the same time. I felt insecure, uncertain, and groundless. Hoping that he would say something that would help me work with these changes, I complained to Trungpa Rinpoche about having trouble with transitions. He looked at me sort of blankly and said, "We are always in transition." Then he said, "If you can just relax with that, you'll have no problem."

We know that all is impermanent; we know that everything wears out. Although we can buy this truth intellectually, emotionally we have a deep-rooted aversion to it. We want permanence; we expect permanence. Our natural tendency is to seek security; we believe we can find it. We experience impermanence at the everyday level as frustration. We use our daily activity as a shield against the fundamental ambiguity of our situation, expending tremendous energy trying to ward off impermanence and death. We don't like it that our bodies change shape. We don't like it that we age. We are afraid of wrinkles and sagging skin. We use health products as if we actually believe that *our* skin, *our* hair, *our* eyes and teeth, might somehow miraculously escape the truth of impermanence.

The Buddhist teachings aspire to set us free from this limited way of relating. They encourage us to relax gradually and wholeheartedly into the ordinary and obvious truth of change. Acknowledging this truth doesn't mean that we're looking on the dark side. What it means is that we begin to understand that we're not the only one who can't keep it all together. We no longer believe that there are people who have managed to avoid uncertainty.

The second mark of existence is egolessness. As human beings we are as impermanent as everything else is. Every cell in the body is continuously changing. Thoughts and emotions rise and fall away unceasingly. When we're thinking that we're competent or that we're hopeless—what are we basing it on? On this fleeting moment? On yesterday's success or failure? We cling to a fixed idea of who we are and it cripples us. Nothing and no one is fixed. Whether the reality of change is a source of freedom for us or a source of horrific anxiety makes a significant difference. Do the days of our lives add up to further suffering or to increased capacity for joy? That's an important question.

Sometimes egolessness is called *no-self*. These words can be misleading. The Buddha was not implying that we disappear—or that we could erase our personality. As a student once asked, "Doesn't experiencing egolessness make life kind of beige?" It's not like that. Buddha was pointing out that the fixed idea that we have about ourselves as solid and separate from each other is painfully limiting. It is possible to move through the drama of our lives without believing so earnestly in the character that we play. That we take ourselves so seriously, that we are so absurdly important in our own minds, is a problem for us. We feel justified in being annoyed with everything. We feel justified in denigrating ourselves or in feeling that we are more clever than other people. Self-importance hurts us, limiting us to the narrow world of our likes and dislikes. We end up bored to death with ourselves and our world. We end up never satisfied.

We have two alternatives: either we question our beliefs—or we don't. Either we accept our fixed versions of reality—or we begin to challenge them. In Buddha's opinion, to train in staying open and curious—to train in dissolving our assumptions and beliefs—is the best use of our human lives.

When we train in awakening bodhichitta, we are nurturing the flexibility of our mind. In the most ordinary terms, egolessness is a flexible identity. It manifests as inquisitiveness, as adaptability, as humor, as playfulness. It is our capacity to relax with not knowing, not figuring everything out, with not being at all sure about who we are—or who anyone else is either.

A man's only son was reported dead in battle. Inconsolable, the father locked himself in his house for three weeks, refusing all support and kindness. In the fourth week the son returned home. Seeing that he was not dead, the people of the village were moved to tears. Overjoyed, they accompanied the young man to his father's house and knocked on the door. "Father," called the son, "I have returned." But the old man refused to answer. "Your son is here, he was not killed," called the people. But the old man would not come to the door. "Go away and leave me to grieve!" he screamed. "I know my son is gone forever and you cannot deceive me with your lies."

So it is with all of us. We are certain about who we are

and who others are and it blinds us. If another version of reality comes knocking on our door, our fixed ideas keep us from accepting it.

How are we going to spend this brief lifetime? Are we going to strengthen our well-perfected ability to struggle against uncertainty, or are we going to train in letting go? Are we going to hold on stubbornly to "I'm like this and you're like that"? Or are we going to move beyond that narrow mind? Could we start to train as a warrior, aspiring to reconnect with the natural flexibility of our being and to help others do the same? If we start to move in this direction, limitless possibilities will begin to open up.

The teaching on egolessness points to our dynamic, changing nature. This body has never felt exactly the way it's feeling now. This mind is thinking a thought that, repetitious as it may seem, will never be thought again. I may say, "Isn't that wonderful?" But we don't usually experience it as wonderful; we experience it as unnerving, and we scramble for ground. The Buddha was generous enough to show us an alternative. We are not trapped in the identity of success or failure, or in any identity at all, neither in terms of how others see us nor in how we see ourselves. Every moment is unique, unknown, completely fresh. For a warrior-in-training, egolessness is a cause of joy rather than a cause of fear.

The third mark of existence is suffering, dissatisfaction. As Suzuki Roshi put it, it is only by practicing through a continual succession of agreeable and disagreeable situations that we acquire true strength. To accept that pain is inherent and to live our lives from this understanding is to create the causes and conditions for happiness.

To put it concisely, we suffer when we resist the noble and irrefutable truth of impermanence and death. We suffer, not because we are basically bad or deserve to be punished, but because of three tragic misunderstandings.

First, we expect that what is always changing should be graspable and predictable. We are born with a craving for resolution and security that governs our thoughts, words, and actions. We are like people in a boat that is falling apart, trying to hold on to the water. The dynamic, energetic, and natural flow of the universe is not acceptable to the conventional mind. Our prejudices and addictions are patterns that arise from the fear of a fluid world. Because we mistakenly take what is always changing to be permanent, we suffer.

Second, we proceed as if we were separate from everything else, as if we were a fixed identity, when our true situation is egoless. We insist on being Someone, with a capital S. We get security from defining ourselves as worthless or worthy, superior or inferior. We waste precious time exaggerating or romanticizing or belittling ourselves with a complacent surety that yes, that's who we are. We mistake the openness of our being—the inherent wonder and surprise of each moment—for a solid, irrefutable self. Because of this misunderstanding, we suffer.

Third, we look for happiness in all the wrong places. The Buddha called this habit "mistaking suffering for happiness," like a moth flying into the flame. As we know, moths are not the only ones who will destroy themselves in order to find temporary relief. In terms of how we seek happiness, we are all like the alcoholic who drinks to stop the depression that escalates with every drink, or the junkie who shoots up in order to get relief from the suffering that increases with every fix.

A friend who is always on a diet pointed out that this teaching would be easier to follow if our addictions *didn't* offer temporary relief. Because we experience short-lived satisfaction from them, we keep getting hooked. In repeating our quest for instant gratification, pursuing addictions of all kinds—some seemingly benign, some obviously lethal—we continue to reinforce old patterns of suffering. We strengthen dysfunctional patterns.

Thus we become less and less able to reside with even the most fleeting uneasiness or discomfort. We become habituated to reaching for something to ease the edginess of the moment. What begins as a slight shift of energy—a minor tightening of our stomach, a vague, indefinable feeling that something bad is about to happen—escalates into addiction. This is our way of trying to make life predictable. Because we mistake what always results in suffering for what will bring us happiness, we remain stuck in the repetitious habit of escalating our dissatisfaction. In Buddhist terminology this vicious cycle is called samsara.

When I begin to doubt that I have what it takes to stay present with impermanence, egolessness, and suffering, it uplifts me to remember Trungpa Rinpoche's cheerful reminder that there is no cure for hot and cold. There is no cure for the facts of life.

This teaching on the three marks of existence can motivate us to stop struggling against the nature of reality. We can stop harming others and ourselves in our efforts to escape the alternation of pleasure and pain. We can relax and be fully present for our lives.

4

Learning to Stay

Meditation practice is regarded as a good
and in fact excellent way to overcome warfare
in the world: our own warfare as well as greater
warfare.

—CHÖGYAM TRUNGPA RINPOCHE

As a species, we should never underestimate our low tolerance for discomfort. To be encouraged to stay with our vulnerability is news that we can use. Sitting meditation is our support for learning how to do this. Sitting meditation, also known as mindfulness-awareness practice, is the foundation of bodhichitta training. It is the natural seat, the home ground of the warrior-bodhisattva.

Sitting meditation cultivates loving-kindness and compassion, the relative qualities of bodhichitta. It gives us a way to move closer to our thoughts and emotions and to get in touch with our bodies. It is a method of cultivating unconditional friendliness toward ourselves and for parting the curtain of indifference that distances us from the suffering of others. It is our vehicle for learning to be a truly loving person.

Gradually, through meditation, we begin to notice that there are gaps in our internal dialogue. In the midst of continually talking to ourselves, we experience a pause, as if awakening from a dream. We recognize our capacity to relax with the clarity, the space, the open-ended awareness that already exists in our minds. We experience moments of being right here that feel simple, direct, and uncluttered.

This coming back to the immediacy of our experience is training in unconditional bodhichitta. By simply staying here, we relax more and more into the open dimension of our being. It feels like stepping out of a fantasy world and discovering the simple truth.

Yet there is no guarantee that sitting meditation will be of benefit. We can practice for years without its penetrating our hearts and minds. We can use meditation to reinforce our false beliefs: it will protect us from discomfort; it will fix us; it will fulfill our hopes and remove our fears. This happens because we don't properly understand why we are practicing.

Why *do* we meditate? This is a question we'd be wise to ask. Why would we even bother to spend time alone with ourselves?

First of all, it is helpful to understand that meditation is not just about feeling good. To think that this is why we meditate is to set ourselves up for failure. We'll assume we are doing it wrong almost every time we sit down: even the most settled meditator experiences psychological and physical pain. Meditation takes us just as we are, with our confusion and our sanity. This complete acceptance of ourselves as we are is called *maitri*, a simple, direct relationship with the way we are.

Trying to fix ourselves is not helpful. It implies struggle and self-denigration. Denigrating ourselves is probably the major way that we cover over bodhichitta.

Does not trying to change mean we have to remain angry and addicted until the day we die? This is a reasonable question. Trying to change ourselves doesn't work in the long run because we're resisting our own energy. Self-improvement can have temporary results, but lasting transformation occurs only when we honor ourselves as the source of wisdom and compassion. We are, as the eighth-century Buddhist master Shantideva pointed out, very much like a blind person who finds a jewel buried in a heap of garbage. Right here in what we'd like to throw away, in what we find repulsive and frightening, we discover the warmth and clarity of bodhichitta.

It is only when we begin to relax with ourselves that meditation becomes a transformative process. Only when we relate with ourselves without moralizing, without harshness, without deception, can we let go of harmful patterns. Without maitri, renunciation of old habits becomes abusive. This is an important point.

There are four qualities of maitri that are cultivated

33

when we meditate: steadfastness, clear seeing, experiencing our emotional distress, and attention to the present moment. These qualities not only apply to sitting meditation but are essential to all the bodhichitta practices and for relating with difficult situations in our daily lives.

Steadfastness. When we practice meditation we are strengthening our ability to be steadfast with ourselves. No matter what comes up—aching bones, boredom, falling asleep, or the wildest thoughts and emotions— we develop a loyalty to our experience. Although plenty of meditators consider it, we don't run screaming out of the room. Instead we acknowledge that impulse as thinking, without labeling it right or wrong. This is no small task. Never underestimate our inclination to bolt when we hurt.

We're encouraged to meditate every day, even for a short time, in order to cultivate this steadfastness with ourselves. We sit under all kinds of circumstances— whether we are feeling healthy or sick, whether we're in a good mood or depressed, whether we feel our meditation is going well or is completely falling apart. As we continue to sit we see that meditation isn't about getting it right or attaining some ideal state. It's about being able to stay present with ourselves. It becomes increasingly clear that we won't be free of self-destructive patterns unless we develop a compassionate understanding of what they are.

One aspect of steadfastness is simply being in your

body. Because meditation emphasizes working with your mind, it's easy to forget that you even have a body. When you sit down it's important to relax into your body and to get in touch with what is going on. Starting with the top of your head, you can spend a few minutes bringing awareness to every part of your body. When you come to places that are hurting or tense you can breathe in and out three or four times, keeping your awareness on that area. When you get to the soles of your feet you can stop, or if you feel like it, you can repeat this body sweep by going from bottom to top. Then at any time during your meditation period, you can quickly tune back in to the overall sense of being in your body. For a moment you can bring your awareness directly back to being right here. You are sitting. There are sounds, smells, sights, aches; you are breathing in and out. You can reconnect with your body like this when it occurs to you—maybe once or twice during a sitting session. Then return to the technique.

In meditation we discover our inherent restlessness. Sometimes we get up and leave. Sometimes we sit there but our bodies wiggle and squirm and our minds go far away. This can be so uncomfortable that we feel it's impossible to stay. Yet this feeling can teach us not just about ourselves but also about what it is to be human. All of us derive security and comfort from the imaginary world of memories and fantasies and plans. We really don't want to stay with the nakedness of our present experience. It goes against the grain to stay present. These are the times when only gentleness and a sense of humor can give us the strength to settle down.

The pith instruction is, Stay . . . stay . . . just stay. Learning to stay with ourselves in meditation is like training a dog. If we train a dog by beating it, we'll end up with an obedient but very inflexible and rather terrified dog. The dog may obey when we say "Stay!" "Come!" "Roll over!" and "Sit up!" but he will also be neurotic and confused. By contrast, training with kindness results in someone who is flexible and confident, who doesn't become upset when situations are unpredictable and insecure.

So whenever we wander off, we gently encourage ourselves to "stay" and settle down. Are we experiencing restlessness? Stay! Discursive mind? Stay! Are fear and loathing out of control? Stay! Aching knees and throbbing back? Stay! What's for lunch? Stay! What am I doing here? Stay! I can't stand this another minute! Stay! That is how to cultivate steadfastness.

Clear seeing. After we've been meditating for a while, it's common to feel that we are regressing rather than waking up. "Until I started meditating, I was quite settled; now it feels like I'm always restless." "I never used to feel anger; now it comes up all the time." We might complain that meditation is ruining our life, but in fact such experiences are a sign that we're starting to see more clearly. Through the process of practicing the technique day in and day out, year after year, we begin to be very honest with ourselves. Clear seeing is another way of saying that we have less self-deception.

The Beat poet Jack Kerouac, feeling primed for a spiritual breakthrough, wrote to a friend before he retreated into the wilderness, "If I don't get a vision on Desolation Peak, then my name ain't William Blake." But later he wrote that he found it hard to face the naked truth. "I'd thought, in June when I get to the top . . . and everybody leaves . . . I will come face to face with God or Tathagata [Buddha] and find out once and for all what is the meaning of all this existence and suffering . . . but instead I'd come face to face with myself, no liquor, no drugs, no chance of faking it, but face to face with ole Hateful . . . Me."

Meditation requires patience and maitri. If this process of clear seeing isn't based on self-compassion it will become a process of self-aggression. We need self-compassion to stabilize our minds. We need it to work with our emotions. We need it in order to stay.

When we learn to meditate, we are instructed to sit in a certain position on a cushion or chair. We're instructed to just be in the present moment, aware of our breath as it goes out. We're instructed that when our mind has wandered off, without any harshness or judgmental quality, we should acknowledge that as "thinking" and return to the outbreath. We train in coming back to this moment of being here. In the process of doing this, our fogginess, our bewilderment, our ignorance begin to transform into clear seeing. *Thinking* becomes a code word for seeing "just what is"—both our clarity and our confusion. We are not trying to get rid of thoughts. Rather, we are clearly seeing our defense mechanisms, our negative beliefs about ourselves, our desires and expectations. We also see our kindness, our bravery, our wisdom.

Through the process of practicing the mindfulness-awareness technique on a regular basis, we can no longer hide from ourselves. We clearly see the barriers we set up to shield us from naked experience. Although we still associate the walls we've erected with safety and comfort, we also begin to feel them as a restriction. This claustrophobic situation is important for a warrior. It marks the beginning of longing for an alternative to our small, familiar world. We begin to look for ventilation. We want to dissolve the barriers between ourselves and others.

Experiencing our emotional distress. Many people, including longtime practitioners, use meditation as a means of escaping difficult emotions. It is possible to misuse the label "thinking" as a way of pushing negativity away. No matter how many times we've been instructed to stay open to whatever arises, we still can use meditation as repression. Transformation occurs only when we remember, breath by breath, year after year, to move toward our emotional distress without condemning or justifying our experience.

Trungpa Rinpoche describes emotion as a combination of self-existing energy and thoughts. Emotion can't proliferate without our internal conversations. If we're angry when we sit down to meditate, we are instructed to label the thoughts "thinking" and let them go. Yet below the thoughts something remains—a vital, pulsating energy. There is nothing wrong, nothing harmful about that underlying energy. Our practice is to stay with it, to experience it, to leave it as it is.

There are certain advanced techniques in which you intentionally churn up emotions by thinking of people or situations that make you angry or lustful or afraid. The practice is to let the thoughts go and connect directly with the energy, asking yourself, "Who am I without these thoughts?" What we do with meditation practice is simpler than that, but I consider it equally daring. When emotional distress arises uninvited, we let the story line go and abide with the energy. This is a felt experience, not a verbal commentary on what is happening. We can feel the energy in our bodies. If we can stay with it, neither acting it out nor repressing it, it wakes us up. People often say, "I fall asleep all the time in meditation. What shall I do?" There are lots of antidotes to drowsiness, but my favorite is, "Experience anger!"

Not abiding with our energy is a predictable human habit. Acting out and repressing are tactics we use to get away from our emotional pain. For instance, most of us when we're angry scream or act it out. We alternate expressions of rage with feeling ashamed of ourselves and wallowing in guilt. We become so stuck in repetitive behavior that we become experts at getting all worked up. In this way we continue to strengthen our painful emotions.

One night years ago I came upon my boyfriend passionately embracing another woman. We were in the house of a friend who had a priceless collection of pottery. I was furious and looking for something to throw. Everything I picked up I had to put back down because it was worth at least ten thousand dollars. I was completely enraged and I couldn't find an outlet! There were no exits from experiencing my own energy. The absurdity of the situation totally cut through my rage. I went outside and looked at the sky and laughed until I cried.

In vajrayana Buddhism it is said that wisdom is inherent in emotions. When we struggle against our energy we reject the source of wisdom. Anger without the fixation is none other than clear-seeing wisdom. Pride without fixation is experienced as equanimity. The energy of passion when it's free of grasping is wisdom that sees all the angles.

In bodhichitta training we also welcome the living energy of emotions. When our emotions intensify, what we usually feel is fear. This fear is always lurking in our lives. In sitting meditation we practice dropping whatever story we are telling ourselves and leaning into the emotions and the fear. Thus we train in opening the fearful heart to the restlessness of our own energy. We learn to abide with the experience of our emotional distress.

Attention to the present moment. Another factor we cultivate in the transformative process of meditation is attention to this very moment. We make the choice, moment by moment, to be fully here. Attending to our present-moment mind and body is a way of being tender toward self, toward other, and toward the world. This quality of attention is inherent in our ability to love.

Coming back to the present moment takes some effort, but the effort is very light. The instruction is to "touch and go." We touch thoughts by acknowledging them as thinking and then we let them go. It's a way of relaxing our struggle, like touching a bubble with a feather. It's a nonaggressive approach to being here.

Sometimes we find that we like our thoughts so much that we don't want to let them go. Watching our internal movie is a lot more entertaining than bringing our mind back home. There's no doubt that our fantasy world can be very juicy and seductive. So we train in using a "soft" effort when interrupting our habitual patterns; in other words, we train in cultivating self-compassion.

We practice meditation to connect with maitri and

unconditional openness. By not deliberately blocking anything, by directly touching our thoughts and then letting them go with an attitude of no big deal, we can discover that our fundamental energy is tender, wholesome, and fresh. We can start to train as a warrior, discovering for ourselves that it is bodhichitta, not confusion, that is basic.

5

Warrior Slogans

> In all activities, train with slogans.
>
> —MIND-TRAINING SLOGAN OF ATISHA

I N THE ELEVENTH CENTURY Atisha Dipankara brought the complete bodhichitta teachings from India to Tibet. In particular he emphasized what are called the *lojong* teachings, the teachings for training the mind. What is so up-to-date about these teachings is that they show us how to transform difficult circumstances into the path of enlightenment; what we most dislike about our lives is the meat and potatoes of the mind-training practices of Atisha. What seem like the greatest obstacles—our anger, our resentment, our uptightness—we use as fuel to awaken bodhichitta.

For some time after the death of Atisha these teachings were kept secret, passed on only to close disciples. They did not become widely known again until the twelfth century, when the Tibetan Geshe Chekawa organized them into fifty-nine pithy slogans. These sayings are now known as the lojong slogans or the slogans of

Atisha. Becoming familiar with these slogans and bringing them to mind throughout our lives is a valuable bodhichitta practice.*

Geshe Chekawa had a brother who was contemptuous of the Buddhist teachings and was always giving him a hard time. However, when many lepers who were studying with Chekawa became cured, his brother began to get very interested in what they were being taught. Hiding outside Chekawa's door, the irascible brother started listening to the teachings on using uncomfortable circumstances as the path. When Chekawa began to notice his brother becoming less irritable, more flexible, and more considerate, he realized that his brother must be listening to the mind-training teachings and applying them. It was then that he decided to teach the lojong slogans far more publicly. He figured that if they could help his brother, they could help anyone.

Ordinarily we are swept away by habitual momentum and don't interrupt our patterns even slightly. When we feel betrayed or disappointed, does it occur to us to practice? Usually not. But right there, in the midst of our confusion, is where the slogans of Atisha are most penetrating. The easy part is to familiarize ourselves with them. More challenging is to remember to apply them. To remember a slogan right in the midst of

---

*For more information on the mind-training slogans, please refer to the appendix, where all fifty-nine slogans are listed, as well as to the list of books on slogan training in the bibliography.

irritation—for example, "Always meditate on whatever provokes resentment"—might cause us to pause before acting out our resentment by saying something mean. Once we are familiar with it, a slogan like this will spontaneously pop into our mind and remind us to stay with the emotional energy rather than acting it out.

The mind-training slogans present us with a challenge. When we are escaping the present moment with a habitual reaction, can we recall a slogan that might bring us back? Rather than spinning off, can we let the emotional intensity of that red-hot or ice-cold moment transform us? The pith of the slogan practice is to take a warrior's attitude toward discomfort. It encourages us to ask, "How can I practice right now, right on this painful spot, and transform this into the path of awakening?" On any average day of our lives, we have plenty of opportunities to ask this question.

The slogan "Train in the three difficulties" gives us instruction on how to practice, how to interrupt our habitual reactions. The three difficulties are (1) acknowledging our neurosis as neurosis, (2) doing something different, and (3) aspiring to continue practicing this way.

Acknowledging that we are all churned up is the first and most difficult step in any practice. Without compassionate recognition that we're stuck, it's impossible to liberate ourselves from confusion. "Doing something different" is anything that interrupts our ancient habit of tenaciously indulging in our emotions. We do anything to cut the strong tendency to spin out. We can let the story line go and connect with the underlying energy or do any of the bodhichitta practices introduced in this book. Anything that's nonhabitual will do—even sing and dance or run around the block. We do anything that doesn't reinforce our crippling habits. The third difficult practice is to then remember that this is not something we do just once or twice. Interrupting our destructive habits and awakening our heart is the work of a lifetime.

In essence the practice is always the same: instead of falling prey to a chain reaction of revenge or self-hatred, we gradually learn to catch the emotional reaction and drop the story lines. Then we feel the bodily sensation completely. One way of doing this is to breathe it into our heart. By acknowledging the emotion, dropping whatever story we are telling ourselves about it, and feeling the energy of the moment, we cultivate compassion for ourselves. Then we could take this a step further. We could recognize that there are millions who are feeling the way we are and breathe in the emotion for all of us with the wish that we could all be free of confusion and limiting habitual reactions. When we can recognize our own confusion with compassion, we can extend that compassion to others who are equally confused. This step of widening the circle of compassion is where the magic of bodhichitta training lies.

The irony is that what we most want to avoid in our lives is crucial to awakening bodhichitta. These juicy emotional spots are where a warrior gains wisdom and compassion. Of course, we'll want to get out of those spots far more often than we'll want to stay. That's why self-compassion and courage are vital. Staying with pain without loving-kindness is just warfare.

When the bottom is falling out we might suddenly recall the slogan "If you can practice even when distracted, you are well trained." If we can practice when we're jealous, resentful, scornful, when we hate ourselves, then we are well trained. Again, practice means not continuing to strengthen the habitual patterns that keep us trapped, doing anything we can to shake up and ventilate our self-justification and blame. We do our best to stay with the strong energy without acting out or repressing. As we do so, our habits become more porous.

Our patterns are well established, seductive, and comforting. Just wishing for them to be ventilated isn't enough. Those of us who struggle with this know. Awareness is the key. Do we see the stories that we're telling ourselves and question their validity? When we are distracted by a strong emotion, do we remember that it is our path? Can we feel the emotion and breathe it into our hearts for ourselves and everyone else? If we can remember to experiment like this even occasionally, we are training as a warrior. And when we can't practice when distracted but *know* that we can't, we are still training well. Never underestimate the power of compassionately recognizing what's going on.

When we're feeling confused about our words and actions and about what does and does not cause harm, out of nowhere the slogan "Of the two witnesses, hold the principal one" might arise. Of the two witnesses—self and other—we're the only one who knows the full truth about ourselves.

Sometimes the way we see our ignorance is by getting feedback from the outside world. Others can be extremely helpful in showing us our blind spots. Particularly if they cause us to wince, we'd be wise to pay attention to their insights and criticism. But ultimately, we are the ones who know what's happening in our hearts and minds. We're the only ones who hear our internal conversations, who know when we withdraw or feel inspired.

When we begin to train we see that we've been pretty ignorant about what we're doing. First, we see that we are rarely able to relax into the present moment. Second, we see that we've fabricated all kinds of strategies to avoid staying present, particularly when we're afraid that whatever's happening will hurt. We also see our strong belief that if only we could do everything right, we'd be able to find a safe, comfortable, and secure place to spend the rest of our lives.

Growing up in the fifties, for a while I believed that what I saw on television sitcoms was the typical family. They all got along. Nobody got drunk or flew into a rage. There was never any real ugliness. Many of us watching thought, of course, that only our family was the exception to the norm. The truth went unspoken in favor of this American dream.

As we practice, we begin to know the difference between our fantasy and reality. The more steadfast we are with our experience, the more aware we become of when we start to tighten and retreat. When we are denigrating ourselves, do we know it? Do we understand where the desire to lash out at another is coming from? Do we aspire not to keep going down that same old self-destructive road? Do we realize that the suffering we feel is shared by all beings? Do we have any longing for all of us to stop sowing the seeds of misery? Only the "principal one" knows the answers to these questions.

We can't expect always to catch ourselves spinning off into a habitual reaction. But as we begin to catch ourselves more frequently and work with interrupting our habitual patterns, we know that the bodhichitta training is seeping in. Our desire to help not just ourselves but all sentient beings will slowly grow.

So in all activities, not just sometimes when things are going well or are particularly bad, train with the bodhichitta slogans of Atisha. But remember, "Don't try to be the fastest," "Abandon any hope of fruition," and "Don't expect applause"!

6

Four Limitless Qualities

May all sentient beings enjoy happiness
and the root of happiness.
May we be free from suffering and the root
of suffering.
May we not be separated from the great
happiness devoid of suffering.
May we dwell in the great equanimity free
from passion, aggression, and prejudice.

—THE FOUR LIMITLESS ONES CHANT

I T'S UP TO US. We can spend our lives cultivating our resentments and cravings or we can explore the path of the warrior—nurturing open-mindedness and courage. Most of us keep strengthening our negative habits and therefore sow the seeds of our own suffering. The bodhichitta practices, however, are ways for us to sow the seeds of well-being. Particularly powerful are the aspiration practices of the four limitless qualities—loving-kindness, compassion, joy, and equanimity.

In these practices we start close to home: we express the wish that we and our loved ones enjoy happiness and be free of suffering. Then we gradually extend that aspiration to a widening circle of relationships. We start just where we are, where the aspirations feel genuine. We begin by acknowledging where we already feel love, compassion, joy, and equanimity. We locate our current experience of these four boundless qualities, however limited they may be: in our love of music, in our empathy with children, in the joy we feel on hearing good news, or in the equanimity we experience when we are with good friends. Even though we may think that what we already experience is too meager, nevertheless we start with that and nurture it. It doesn't have to be grand.

Cultivating these four qualities gives us insight into our current experience. It gives us understanding of the state of our mind and heart right now. We get to know the experience of love and compassion, of joy and equanimity, and also of their opposites. We learn how it feels when one of the four qualities is stuck and how it feels when it is flowing freely. We never pretend that we feel anything we don't. The practice depends on embracing our whole experience. By becoming intimate with how we close down and how we open up, we awaken our unlimited potential.

Even though we start this practice with the aspiration for ourselves or our loved ones to be free of suffering, it may feel as if we're just mouthing words. Even this compassionate wish for those nearest to us may feel phony. But as long as we're not deceiving ourselves, this pretending has the power to uncover bodhichitta. Even though we know exactly what we feel, we make the aspirations in order to move beyond what now seems possible. After we practice for ourselves and those near us, we stretch even further: we send goodwill toward the neutral people in our lives and also to the people we don't like.

It might feel like stretching into make-believe to say, "May this person who is driving me crazy enjoy happiness and be free of suffering." Probably what we genuinely feel is anger. This practice is like a workout that stretches the heart beyond its current capabilities. We can expect to encounter resistance. We discover that we have our limits: we can stay open to some people, but we remain closed to others. We see both our clarity and our confusion. We are learning firsthand what everyone who has ever set out on this path has learned: we are all a paradoxical bundle of rich potential that consists of both neurosis and wisdom.

Aspiration practice is different from making affirmations. Affirmations are like telling yourself that you are compassionate and brave in order to hide the fact that secretly you feel like a loser. In practicing the four limitless qualities, we aren't trying to convince ourselves of anything, nor are we trying to hide our true feelings. We are expressing our willingness to open our hearts and move closer to our fears.

Aspiration practice helps us to do this in increasingly difficult relationships.

If we acknowledge the love, compassion, joy, and equanimity that we feel now and nurture it through these practices, the expansion of those qualities will happen by itself. Awakening the four qualities provides the necessary warmth for an unlimited strength to emerge. They have the power to loosen up useless habits and to melt the ice-hardness of our fixations and defenses. We are not forcing ourselves to be good. When we see how cold or aggressive we can be, we aren't asking ourselves to repent. Rather, these aspiration practices develop our ability to remain steadfast with our experience, whatever it may be. In this way we come to know the difference between a closed and an open mind, gradually developing the self-awareness and kindness we need to benefit others. These practices unblock our love and compassion, joy and equanimity, tapping into their boundless potential to expand.

7

Loving-Kindness

> Peace between countries must rest on the solid
> foundation of love between individuals.
>
> —MAHATMA GANDHI

OUR PERSONAL ATTEMPTS to live humanely in
this world are never wasted. Choosing to cultivate love rather than anger just might be what it takes
to save the planet from extinction.

What is it that allows our goodwill to expand and
our prejudice and anger to decrease? This is a significant question. Traditionally it is said that the root of aggression and suffering is ignorance. But what is it that
we are ignoring? Entrenched in the tunnel vision of our
personal concerns, what we ignore is our kinship with
others. One reason we train as warrior-bodhisattvas
is to recognize our interconnectedness—to grow in
understanding that when we harm another, we are
harming ourselves. So we train in recognizing our
uptightness. We train in seeing that others are not

so different from ourselves. We train in opening our hearts and minds in increasingly difficult situations.

For an aspiring bodhisattva, the essential practice is to cultivate maitri. In the Shambhala teachings this is called "placing our fearful mind in the cradle of loving-kindness." Another image for maitri or loving-kindness is that of a mother bird who protects and cares for her young until they are strong enough to fly away. People sometimes ask, "Who am I in this image—the mother or the chicks?" The answer is we're both: both the loving mother and those ugly little chicks. It's easy to identify with the babies—blind, raw, and desperate for attention. We are a poignant mixture of something that isn't all that beautiful and yet is dearly loved. Whether this is our attitude toward ourselves or toward others, it is the key to learning how to love. We stay with ourselves and others when we're screaming for food and have no feathers and also when we are more grown up and more cute by worldly standards.

In cultivating loving-kindness, we train first to be honest, loving, and compassionate toward ourselves. Rather than nurturing self-denigration, we begin to cultivate a clear-seeing kindness. Sometimes we feel good and strong. Sometimes we feel inadequate and weak. But like mother love, maitri is unconditional. No matter how we feel, we can aspire to be happy. We can learn to act and think in ways that sow seeds of our future well-being, gradually becoming more aware of what causes happiness as well as what causes distress.

Without loving-kindness for ourselves, it is difficult, if not impossible, to genuinely feel it for others.

To move from aggression to unconditional loving-kindness can seem like a daunting task. But we start with what's familiar. The instruction for cultivating limitless maitri is to first find the tenderness that we already have. We touch in with our gratitude or appreciation—our current ability to feel goodwill. In a very nontheoretical way we contact the soft spot of bodhichitta. Whether we find it in the tenderness of feeling love or the vulnerability of feeling lonely is immaterial. If we look for that soft, unguarded place, we can always find it.

For instance, even in the rock-hardness of rage, if we look below the surface of the aggression, we'll generally find fear. There's something beneath the solidity of anger that feels very raw and sore. Underneath the defensiveness is the brokenhearted, unshielded quality of bodhichitta. Rather than feel this tenderness, however, we tend to close down and protect against the discomfort. That we close down is not a problem. In fact, to become aware of when we do so is an important part of the training. The first step in cultivating loving-kindness is to see when we are erecting barriers between ourselves and others. This compassionate recognition is essential. Unless we understand—in a nonjudgmental way—that we are hardening our hearts, there is no possibility of dissolving that armor. Without dissolving the armor, the loving-kindness of bodhichitta is always held back. We are always obstructing our innate capacity to love without an agenda.

So we train in awakening the loving-kindness of bodhichitta in all kinds of relationships, both open-hearted and blocked. All these relationships become aids in uncovering our ability to feel and express love.

The formal practice of loving-kindness or maitri has seven stages.* We begin by engendering loving-kindness for ourselves and then expand it at our own pace to include loved ones, friends, "neutral" persons, those who irritate us, all of the above as a group, and finally, all beings throughout time and space. We gradually widen the circle of loving-kindness.

The traditional aspiration used is "May I and others enjoy happiness and the root of happiness." In teaching this I've found that people sometimes have trouble with the word *happiness*. They say things like, "Suffering has taught me a lot and happiness gets me in trouble." They aren't sure that happiness is what they wish for themselves or others. This may be because our conventional notion of happiness is far too limited.

To get at the heart of the loving-kindness practice we may have to put the aspiration for happiness into our own words. One man told me of his aspiration that he and others realize their fullest potential. The aspiration of a woman I know is that we all learn to speak and think and act in a way that adds up to fundamental

---

*See the appendix for a concise overview.

well-being. The aspiration of another person is that all beings—including himself—begin to trust in their basic goodness. It is important that each of us make the aspiration as genuine as possible.

To work with this practice it is useful to consider ahead of time people or animals for whom we already feel good heart. This might be a feeling of gratitude or appreciation or a feeling of tenderness. Any feeling of genuine heart will do. If it's helpful, we can even start a list of those who easily inspire these feelings.

Traditionally we begin the practice with ourselves, but sometimes people find that too hard. It's important to include ourselves, but whom we start with isn't critical. The point is to contact an honest feeling of goodwill and encourage it to expand. If you can easily open your heart to your dog or cat, start there and then move out to more challenging relationships. The practice is about connecting with the soft spot in a way that is real to us, not about faking a particular feeling. Just locate that ability to feel good heart and cherish it, even if it ebbs and flows.

Before we begin the aspiration practice we sit quietly for a few minutes. Then we begin the seven-step loving-kindness practice. We say, "May I (or a loved one) enjoy happiness and the root of happiness," or we put that in our own words. Perhaps we say, "May we learn to be truly loving people." Or "May we have enough to eat and a place to sleep where we will be safe and comfortable."

After making this aspiration for ourselves and for someone we easily love, we move on to a friend. This relationship should be slightly more complicated. For example, we care for her but perhaps we also feel jealous. We say, "May Jane enjoy happiness and the root of happiness." And we send loving-kindness her way. We can spend as much time as we want with each stage of this process, not criticizing ourselves if we sometimes find it artificial or contrived.

The fourth step is to cultivate loving-kindness for a neutral person. This would be someone we encounter but don't really know. We don't feel one way or another toward this person. We say, "May the shopkeeper (the bus driver, the woman who lives down the hall, the panhandler on the street) enjoy happiness and the root of happiness." Then we watch without judgment to see if our heart opens or closes down. We practice awareness of when tenderness is blocked and when it is flowing freely.

The Buddhist teachings tell us that over the course of many lifetimes all beings have been our mothers. At one time, all these people have sacrificed their own comfort for our well-being, and vice versa. Although these days "mother" doesn't always have a positive connotation, the point is to consider everyone we encounter as our beloved. By noticing and appreciating the people in the streets, at the grocery store, in traffic jams, in airports, we can increase our capacity to love. We use these aspirations to weaken the barriers of indifference and liberate the good heart of loving-kindness.

The fifth step of the maitri practice is to work with a difficult person, someone we find irritating; when we see this person we armor our heart. We continue as before by making the loving-kindness aspiration. "May this really annoying person enjoy happiness and the root of happiness. May this woman whom I resent awaken bodhichitta." It's best, at least at the beginning, not to practice with our heaviest relationships. If we jump right into the traumas of our lives, we'll feel overwhelmed. Then we'll begin to fear the practice and walk away. So in this fifth stage we work with the feeling of negativity, but not the most heavy-duty variety. If we start with less-difficult relationships first, we can trust that our capacity to stay open to people we dislike will gradually expand by itself.

Because they challenge us to the limits of our open-mindedness, difficult relationships are in many ways the most valuable for practice. The people who irritate us are the ones who inevitably blow our cover. Through them we might come to see our defenses very clearly. Shantideva explained it like this: If we wish to practice generosity and a beggar arrives, that's good news. The beggar gives us an opportunity to learn how to give. Likewise, if we want to practice patience and unconditional loving-kindness and an enemy arrives, we are in luck. Without the ones who irritate us, we never have a chance to practice.

Before Atisha brought the bodhichitta practices from India to Tibet, he was told that the people in Tibet were universally cheerful and kind. He was afraid that if this was the case, he'd have no one to provoke him and show him where he needed to train. So he chose to bring along the most difficult person in his life—his Bengali tea boy, who was as skillful at showing him his faults as his guru. The joke is that he really didn't need that Bengali servant. There were already plenty of irritating people in Tibet.

The sixth stage of the practice is called "completely dissolving the barriers." We visualize ourselves, our beloved, a friend, a neutral person, and our current Bengali tea person—all standing in front of us. At this stage we try to connect with the feeling of kind heart for all these individuals. We evoke equal loving-kindness for the loved ones and the enemies in our lives, as well as for those who evoke indifference. We say, "May each of us equally enjoy happiness and the root of happiness." Or again, we can put this in our own words.

The seventh and final stage is to expand loving-kindness to all beings. We extend our aspiration as far as we can. We can start with those nearby and gradually widen our circle to include the neighborhood, the city, the nation, and the universe. "May all beings in the universe enjoy happiness and its causes." This is equivalent to making the aspiration that the whole universe be at peace.

Each stage of the practice gives us a further chance

to loosen up the tightness of our hearts. It's fine to take just one stage and work with that for a while. In fact, many people train in the first stage for a week or more, aspiring over and over that they themselves enjoy happiness and its cause. We can also simplify the stages. One form of loving-kindness practice has just these three steps: "May I enjoy happiness and its causes. May you enjoy happiness and its causes. May all beings everywhere be happy."

At the end of the loving-kindness practice, we drop all the words, all the wishes, and simply come back to the nonconceptual simplicity of sitting meditation.

The main point of doing this practice is to uncover the ability to love without bias. Making the aspirations is like watering the seed of goodwill so it can begin to grow. In the course of doing this we'll become acquainted with our barriers—numbness, inadequacy, skepticism, resentment, righteous indignation, pride, and all the others. As we continue to do this practice, we make friends with our fears, our grasping, and our aversion. Unconditional good heart toward others is not even a possibility unless we attend to our own demons. Everything we encounter thus becomes an opportunity for practicing loving-kindness.

8

Compassion

> In other traditions demons are expelled
> externally. But in my tradition demons are
> accepted with compassion.

> —MACHIK LABDRÖN

J UST AS NURTURING our ability to love is a way
of awakening bodhichitta, so also is nurturing our
ability to feel compassion. Compassion, however, is
more emotionally challenging than loving-kindness
because it involves the willingness to feel pain. It definitely requires the training of a warrior.

For arousing compassion, the nineteenth-century
yogi Patrul Rinpoche suggested imagining beings
in torment—an animal about to be slaughtered, a
person awaiting execution. To make it more immediate, he recommended imagining ourselves in their
place. Particularly painful is his image of a mother
with no arms watching as a raging river sweeps her
child away. To contact the suffering of another being
fully and directly is as painful as being in that woman's

shoes. For most of us, even to consider such a thing is frightening. When we practice generating compassion, we can expect to experience our fear of pain. Compassion practice is daring. It involves learning to relax and allow ourselves to move gently toward what scares us. The trick to doing this is to stay with emotional distress without tightening into aversion, to let fear soften us rather than harden into resistance.

It can be difficult to even think about beings in torment, let alone to act on their behalf. Recognizing this, we begin with a practice that is fairly easy. We cultivate bravery through making aspirations. We make the wish that all beings, including ourselves and those we dislike, be free of suffering and the root of suffering.

We use the same seven-step aspiration practice to soften our hearts and also to become more honest and forgiving about when and how we shut down. Without justifying or condemning ourselves, we do the courageous work of opening to suffering. This can be the pain that comes when we put up barriers or the pain of opening our heart to our own sorrow or that of another being. We learn as much about doing this from our failures as we do from our successes. In cultivating compassion we draw from the wholeness of our experience—our suffering, our empathy, as well as our cruelty and terror. It has to be this way. Compassion is not a relationship between the healer and the wounded. It's a relationship between equals. Only when we know our own darkness well can we be present with the darkness of others. Compassion becomes real when we recognize our shared humanity.

As in the loving-kindness practice, we start the compassion practice where we are and then expand our capacity. We start by locating our current ability to be genuinely touched by suffering. We make a list of those who evoke a feeling of compassion. It might include our grandchild and our brother and our friend who is afraid of dying, beings we see on the news or read about in a book. The point is simply to contact genuine compassion, wherever we may find it.

To start the formal compassion practice, we begin as before with a period of silent meditation. Then we begin the seven aspirations. Starting with ourselves, we make the traditional aspiration: "May I be free of suffering and the root of suffering." In order for the process to feel genuine, we can put this into our own words. It's important that the aspiration doesn't feel sentimental or contrived.

Thich Nhat Hanh suggests these alternatives: "May I be safe and free from accidents. May I be free of anger, . . . fear, and worries. May I not fall into a state of indifference or be caught in the extremes of craving and aversion. May I not be the victim of self-deception."

After cultivating compassion for ourselves we move on to someone on our list: "May laboratory animals be free of suffering. May my teenage nephew free himself from heroin addiction. May my grandfather in the nursing home not be so lonely and afraid." The point is not to become overwhelmed but simply to contact genuine compassion. ·

The third step is visualizing a friend and cultivating the intention that he or she not have to suffer. This can be the formal aspiration that our friend be free of suffering and the roots of suffering, or it can be something more specific: "May Jack stop holding a grudge against his brother. May Maria be free of her unrelenting physical pain." Then we up the ante by moving on to the neutral people and those whom we dislike.

The neutral people of the fourth stage present an interesting challenge. Many of us come to this point of the practice and go numb. We say the aspiration but can't connect with people we don't know. We might be shocked to find how indifferent or even fearful we are toward so many people. Particularly if we live in a city, there are thousands of people whom we ignore every day. For this reason, I find it particularly important to make aspirations for the so-called neutrals. When we look at someone on the street and wish her to be free of suffering, that person begins to come into focus. We can actually feel the barriers come down. By making this compassionate aspiration, we start to free ourselves from the prison of isolation and indifference.

In the fifth stage, when we generate compassion for the difficult people in our lives, we get to see our prejudices and aversions even more clearly. It can feel completely unreasonable to make a compassionate wish for these irritating, belligerent people. To wish that those we dislike and fear would not suffer can feel like too big a leap. This is a good time to remember that when we harden our heart against anyone, we hurt ourselves. The fear habit, the anger habit, the self-pity habit—all are strengthened and empowered when we continue to buy into them. The most compassionate thing we can do is to interrupt these habits. Instead of always pulling back and putting up walls, we can do something unpredictable and make a compassionate aspiration. We can visualize this difficult person's face and say his name if it helps us. Then we say the words: "May this person who irritates me be free of suffering and the roots of suffering." By doing this, we start to dissolve our fear. We make this gesture of compassion in order to unblock our ability to hear the cries of the world.

The sixth stage is where we make a compassionate aspiration for ourselves, the loved one, the friend, the neutral, and the difficult one all together. This is how we train in lightening up the opinions and prejudices that set us apart from each other. We voice the aspiration that all of us equally be free of suffering and its causes. We then extend our wish further and further, wishing that all beings without exception be free of suffering and the root of suffering—wishing that all beings no longer be captured by their prejudices.

As a result of compassion practice, we will start to have a deeper understanding of the roots of suffering. We wish not only that the outer manifestations of suffering will decrease but also that all of us could stop acting and thinking in ways that escalate ignorance and confusion. We aspire to be free of fixation and closed-mindedness. We wish to dissolve the myth that we are separate.

It is said that all beings are predisposed to waking up and reaching out to others and that this natural inclination can be nurtured. This is what we are doing when we make the aspirations. If we do not cultivate these inclinations, however, they will diminish. Bodhichitta is like a yeast that never loses potency. Any time we add the moisture and warmth of compassion, it will automatically expand. If we keep it in the freezer, however, nothing happens.

I find it particularly helpful to take the compassionate aspirations into the marketplace. I like to do these practices right in the midst of this paradoxical, unpredictable world. In this way I work with my intention but I also begin to act. In traditional terms, this is cultivating both the aspiration and the action levels of bodhichitta. Sometimes this is the only way to make this practice feel relevant to the suffering we continually witness.

Standing in the checkout line, I might notice the defiant teenager in front of me and make the aspiration, "May he be free of suffering and its causes." In the elevator with a stranger, I might notice her shoes, her hands, the expression on her face. I contemplate the fact that just like me she doesn't want stress in her life. Just like me she has worries. Through our hopes and fears, our pleasures and pains, we are deeply inter-connected. I do this sort of thing in all kinds of situa-tions—at the breakfast table, in the meditation hall, at the dentist's office.

When I practice the aspirations on the spot, I no longer feel so separated from others. When I read in the news that someone I don't know was in a car crash, I try not to just pass on to the next article. I generate compassion for her and her family as if she were my best friend. Even more challenging is to make these aspirations for someone who has been violent toward others.

The aspiration practices of the four qualities are training in not holding back, training in seeing our biases and not feeding them. Gradually we will get the hang of going beyond our fear of feeling pain. This is what it takes to become involved with the sorrows of the world, to extend love and compassion, joy and equanimity to everyone—no exceptions.

A teacher once told me that if I wanted lasting hap-piness, the only way to get it was to step out of my cocoon. When I asked her how to bring happiness to others, she said, "Same instruction." This is the reason that I work with these aspiration practices: the best way to serve ourselves is to love and care for others. These are powerful tools for dissolving the barriers that perpetuate not just our own unhappiness, but the suffering of all beings.

9
Tonglen

In joy and sorrow all are equal,
Thus be guardian of all, as of yourself.

—SHANTIDEVA

Tonglen, or exchanging oneself for others, is another bodhichitta practice for activating loving-kindness and compassion. In Tibetan the word *tonglen* literally means "sending and taking." It refers to being willing to take in the pain and suffering of ourselves and others and to send out happiness to us all. The bodhichitta teachings that Atisha took to Tibet included the practice of tonglen.

Although there are many ways that we can approach tonglen, the essence of the practice is always the same. We breathe in what is painful and unwanted with the sincere wish that we and others could be free of suffering. As we do so, we drop the story line that goes along with the pain and feel the underlying energy. We completely open our hearts and minds to whatever arises. Exhaling, we send out relief from the pain with the intention that we and others be happy.

When we are willing to stay even a moment with uncomfortable energy, we gradually learn not to fear it. Then when we see someone in distress we're not reluctant to breathe in the person's suffering and send out relief.

The formal practice of tonglen has four stages. The first stage is a brief moment of stillness or openness— a moment of unconditional bodhichitta. The second stage is visualizing and working with the texture, the raw energy, of claustrophobia and spaciousness. The third stage is the essence of the practice: breathing in whatever is unwanted and breathing out a sense of relief. In the fourth stage we extend our compassion further by including others who are experiencing the same feelings. If we want, we can combine the third stage and the fourth stage, breathing in and out for self and other at the same time.

So the first stage of tonglen is a moment of open mind, or unconditional bodhichitta. Although this stage is crucial, it is difficult to describe. It relates to the Buddhist teaching of shunyata—often translated as "emptiness" or "openness." Experiencing shunyata at an emotional level, we might feel as if we were big enough to accommodate everything, that there's no place for things to get stuck. If we relax our mind and stop struggling, emotions can move through us without becoming solid and proliferating.

Fundamentally, experiencing openness is having trust in the living quality of basic energy. We develop the confidence to allow it to arise, to linger, and then to pass on. This energy is dynamic, ungraspable, always in a state of flux. So our training is, first of all, noticing how we block the energy or freeze it, how we tense up our bodies and minds. Then we train in softening, relaxing, and opening to the energy without interpretations or judgments.

The first flash of openness reminds us that we can always let go of our fixed ideas and connect with something open, fresh, and unbiased. Then, during the following stages, when we begin to breathe in the energy of claustrophobia and unwanted feelings, we breathe them into that huge space, as vast as the clear blue sky. Then we send out whatever we can to help all of us experience the freedom of an open, flexible mind. The longer we practice, the more accessible this unconditional space will be. Sooner or later we are going to realize that we are already awake.

Many of us have no idea what flashing openness is supposed to feel like. The first time I recognized it was simple and direct. In the hall where I was meditating a large fan hummed loudly. After a while I no longer noticed the sound, it was so ongoing. But then the fan abruptly stopped and there was a gap, a wide-open silence. That was my introduction to shunyata!

To flash openness, some people visualize a vast ocean or a cloudless sky—any image that conveys unlimited expansiveness. In group practice, a gong is rung at the beginning. Just listening to the sound of the gong can act as a reminder of open mind. The flash is relatively short, no longer than it takes for a gong to stop resonating. We can't hold on to such an experience. We just touch it briefly and then go on.

In the second stage of tonglen we begin to breathe in the qualities of claustrophobia: thick, heavy, and hot. We might visualize the claustrophobia as coal dust or as yellow-brown smog. Then we breathe out the qualities of spaciousness: fresh, light, and cool. We might visualize this as brilliant moonlight, as sparkling sun on water, as the colors of a rainbow.

However we visualize these textures, we imagine breathing them in and out through all the pores of our body, not only through our mouth and nose. We do this until it feels synchronized with our breath and we are clear about what we are taking in and what we're sending out. It's fine to breathe a little more deeply than usual, but it's important to give the inbreath and the outbreath equal time.

We may find, however, that we favor the inbreath or the outbreath instead of keeping them balanced. For example, we may not want to interrupt the freshness and brightness of the outbreath by taking in what's thick, heavy, and hot. As a result the outbreath may be long and generous, the inbreath short and stingy. Or, we may have no trouble connecting with claustrophobia on the inbreath but feel we don't have much to send out. Then our outbreath may be nearly non-existent. If we feel poverty-stricken like this, we can remember that what we send is not our personal possession. We are simply opening to the space that is always here and sharing it.

In stage three, we start doing the exchange for a specific person. We breathe in this person's pain and we send out relief. Traditionally, the instruction is to begin doing tonglen for the ones who spontaneously spark our compassion, such as those we put on our list. As we breathe in we visualize our hearts opening wide to accept the pain. As we breathe out we send that bravery and openness. We don't cling to it, thinking, "Finally I have a little relief in my life; I want to keep it forever!" Instead, we share it. When we practice like this, breathing in becomes opening and accepting what is unwanted; breathing out becomes letting go and opening even further. Breathing in or breathing out, we are reversing ancient habits of closing to pain and clinging to anything comforting.

Some AIDS hospices encourage patients to do tonglen for others who have AIDS. This connects them in a very real way with everyone in their situation and helps to relieve their shame, fear, and isolation. Hospice workers do tonglen to create an atmosphere of clarity so that the people around them can find their courage and inspiration and be free of fear.

Doing tonglen for another person ventilates our very limited personal reference point, the closed-mindedness that is the source of so much pain. To train in releasing our tight hold on self and to care for others is what connects us with the soft spot of bodhichitta. That's why we do tonglen. We do the practice whenever there is suffering—either ours or others'. After a while it becomes impossible to know whether we are practicing for our own benefit or for the benefit of others. These distinctions begin to break down.

For example, perhaps we are practicing tonglen because we want to help our ailing mother. But somehow our own reactive emotions—guilt, fear, or pent-up anger—arise and seem to block a genuine exchange. At that point we can shift our focus and start breathing in our conflicted feelings, using our personal pain as a link with other people who feel shut down and afraid. Opening our hearts to stuck emotions has the power to clear the air and also benefit our mother.

Sometimes we might not know what to send on the outbreath. We can send something generic, like spaciousness and relief or loving-kindness, or we can send something specific and concrete, like a bouquet of flowers. For example, a woman who was practicing tonglen for her schizophrenic father had no difficulty breathing in with the wish for him to be free of suffering. But she would get stuck on the outbreath, because she had no idea of what to send him that could help. Finally, she came up with the idea of sending him a good cup of coffee, one of his favorite pleasures. The point is to use whatever works.

The practice is about opening to whatever arises, but it's important not to be overly ambitious. We aspire to keep our hearts open in the present moment, but we know it won't always be possible. We can trust that if we just do tonglen as best we presently can, our ability to feel compassion will gradually expand.

When we are practicing tonglen for a specific individual, we always include the fourth stage, which is extending the compassion to everyone in the same predicament. For example, if we are doing tonglen for our sister who has lost her husband, we can breathe in the suffering of other people who are grieving for lost loved ones and send them all relief. If we are practicing for an abused child, we can breathe in and out for all frightened, unprotected children and expand it even further to all beings who are living in terror. If we are doing tonglen with our own pain, we always remember those who have similar anguish and include them as we breathe in and breathe out. In other words, we start with something particular and genuine and then widen the circle as far as we can.

I recommend using tonglen as an on-the-spot practice. Doing tonglen throughout our day can feel more natural than doing it on the cushion. For one thing, there is never any lack of subject matter. When a strong unwanted feeling arises or we see someone hurting, there is nothing theoretical about what we'll use to practice. There are no four stages to remember and no struggle to synchronize textures with the breath. Right there when it's very real and immediate we breathe in and out with the pain. Daily-life practice is never abstract. As soon as uncomfortable emotions come up, we train ourselves in breathing them in and dropping the story line. At the same time, we extend our thoughts and concern to other people who feel the same discomfort, and we breathe in with the wish that all of us could be free of this particular brand of confusion. Then, as we breathe out, we send ourselves and others whatever kind of relief we think would help. We also practice like this when we encounter animals and people who are in pain. We can try to do this whenever difficult situations and feelings arise, and over time it will become more automatic.

It is also helpful to notice anything in our daily life that brings us happiness. As soon as we become aware of it, we can think of sharing it with others, further cultivating the tonglen attitude.

As warrior-bodhisattvas, the more we train in cultivating this attitude, the more we uncover our capacity for joy and equanimity. Because of our bravery and willingness to work with the practice, we are more able to experience the basic goodness of ourselves and others. We're more able to appreciate the potential of all kinds of people: those we find pleasant, those we find unpleasant, and those we don't even know. Thus tonglen begins to ventilate our prejudices and introduce us to a more tender and open-minded world.

Trungpa Rinpoche used to say, however, that there

are no guarantees when we practice tonglen. We have to answer our own questions. Does it really alleviate suffering? Aside from helping us, does it also benefit others? If someone on the other side of the earth is hurting, will it help her that somebody cares? Tonglen is not all that metaphysical. It's simple and very human. We can do it and discover for ourselves what happens.

10

Finding the Ability to Rejoice

> Let the flower of compassion blossom in the
> rich soil of maitri, and water it with the good
> water of equanimity in the cool, refreshing
> shade of joy.

— LONGCHENPA

As we train in the bodhichitta practices, we gradually feel more joy, the joy that comes from a growing appreciation of our basic goodness. We still experience strong conflicting emotions, we still experience the illusion of separateness, but there's a fundamental openness that we begin to trust. This trust in our fresh, unbiased nature brings us unlimited joy— a happiness that's completely devoid of clinging and craving. This is the joy of happiness without a hangover.

How do we cultivate the conditions for joy to expand? We train in staying present. In sitting meditation, we train in mindfulness and maitri: in being steadfast with our bodies, our emotions, our thoughts.

We stay with our own little plot of earth and trust that it can be cultivated, that cultivation will bring it to its full potential. Even though it's full of rocks and the soil is dry, we begin to plow this plot with patience. We let the process evolve naturally.

At the beginning joy is just a feeling that our own situation is workable. We stop looking for a more suitable place to be. We've discovered that the continual search for something better does not work out. This doesn't mean that there are suddenly flowers growing where before there were only rocks. It means we have confidence that something will grow here.

As we cultivate our garden, the conditions become more conducive to the growth of bodhichitta. The joy comes from not giving up on ourselves, from mindfully sticking with ourselves and beginning to experience our great warrior spirit. We also provide the conditions for joy to expand by training in the practices of the heart, and in particular by training in rejoicing and appreciation. As with the other limitless qualities, we can do this as a seven-stage aspiration practice.

A traditional aspiration for awakening appreciation and joy is "May I and others never be separated from the great happiness that is devoid of suffering." This refers to always abiding in the wide-open, unbiased nature of our minds—to connecting with the inner strength of basic goodness. To do this, however, we start with conditioned examples of good fortune such as health, basic intelligence, a supportive environment—

the fortunate conditions that constitute a precious human birth. For the awakening warrior, the greatest advantage is to find ourselves in a time when it is possible to hear and practice the bodhichitta teachings. We are doubly blessed if we have a spiritual friend—a more accomplished warrior—to guide us.

We can practice the first step of the aspiration by learning to rejoice in our own good fortune. We can train in rejoicing in even the smallest blessings our life holds. It is easy to miss our own good fortune; often happiness comes in ways we don't even notice. It's like a cartoon I saw of an astonished-looking man saying, "What was that?" The caption below read, "Bob experiences a moment of well-being." The ordinariness of our good fortune can make it hard to catch.

The key is to be here, fully connected with the moment, paying attention to the details of ordinary life. By taking care of ordinary things—our pots and pans, our clothing, our teeth—we rejoice in them. When we scrub a vegetable or brush our hair, we are expressing appreciation: friendship toward ourselves and toward the living quality that is found in everything. This combination of mindfulness and appreciation connects us fully with reality and brings us joy. When we extend attention and appreciation toward our environment and other people, our experience of joy gets even bigger.

In the Zen tradition, students are taught to bow to other people as well as ordinary objects as a way of expressing their respect. They are taught to take equal care of brooms and toilets and plants in order to show their gratitude to these things. Watching Trungpa Rinpoche set the table for breakfast one morning was like watching someone arrange flowers or create a stage set. He took such care and delight in placing every detail—the place mats and napkins; the forks, knives, and spoons; the plates and the coffee cups. It took him several hours to complete the task! Since then, even though I usually have only a few minutes, I appreciate the ritual of setting the table as an opportunity to be present and rejoice.

Rejoicing in ordinary things is not sentimental or trite. It actually takes guts. Each time we drop our complaints and allow everyday good fortune to inspire us, we enter the warrior's world. We can do this even at the most difficult moments. Everything we see, hear, taste, and smell has the power to strengthen and uplift us. As Longchenpa says, the quality of joy is like finding cool, refreshing shade.

The second stage in learning to rejoice is to think of a loved one and to appreciate his or her good fortune. We start with a person we feel good about. We can imagine the loved one's face or say the person's name if it makes the practice more real. Then in our own words, we rejoice—that a person who was ill is now feeling healthy and cheerful, that a child who was lonely has found a friend. We are encouraged to try to keep it simple. The point is to find our spontaneous and natural capacity to be glad for another being, whether it feels unshakable or fleeting.

In the next three stages of the practice, as we practice with people less dear to us, our ability to appreciate and rejoice in their good fortune is frequently blocked by envy or other emotions. This is an important point for the bodhisattva-in-training. Our practice is to become aware of our kind heart and nurture it. But it is also to get a close look at the roots of suffering—to see the way we close our hearts with emotions such as jealousy. I find the rejoicing practice an especially powerful tool for doing this.

What happens when we make the gesture to rejoice for the good fortune of our neighbor? We might say the words "I rejoice that Henry won the lottery," but what is happening in our hearts and minds? When we say, "I rejoice that Tania has a boyfriend," how do we really feel? The aspiration to rejoice can feel feeble compared with our resentment or envy or self-pity. We know how easy it is to let emotions hook us in and shut us down. We'd be wise to question why we hold a grudge as if it were going to make us happy and ease our pain. It's rather like eating rat poison and thinking the rat will die. Our desire for relief and the methods we use to achieve it are definitely not in sync.

Whenever we get caught, it's helpful to remember the teachings—to recall that suffering is the result of an aggressive mind. Even slight irritation causes us pain when we indulge in it. This is the time to ask,

"Why am I doing this to myself again?" Contemplating the causes of suffering right on the spot empowers us. We begin to recognize that we have what it takes to cut through our habit of eating poison. Even if it takes the rest of our lives, nevertheless, we can do it.

When we work with neutral people, what happens to our hearts? We say the words in our practice or out on the street, "I rejoice for that man sitting comfortably in the sun." "I am glad for the dog that was adopted at the pound." We say the words and what happens? When we regard others with appreciation, do the barriers go up or do they come down?

Difficult people are, as usual, the greatest teachers. Aspiring to rejoice in their good fortune is a good opportunity to investigate our reactions and our strategies. How do we react to their good luck, good health, good news? With envy? With anger? With fear? What is our strategy for moving away from what we feel? Revenge, self-denigration? What stories do we tell ourselves? ("She's a snob." "I'm a failure.") These reactions, strategies, and story lines are what cocoons and prison walls are made of.

Then, right on the spot, we can go beneath the words to the nonverbal experience of the emotion. What's happening in our hearts, our shoulders, our gut? Abiding with the physical sensation is radically different from sticking to the story line. It requires appreciation for this very moment. It is a way of relaxing, a way to train in softening rather than hardening.

It allows the ground of limitless joy—basic goodness—to shine through.

Can we now rejoice for ourselves, our loved one, friend, the neutral, the difficult one, all together? Can we rejoice for all beings throughout time and space?

"Always maintain only a joyful mind" is one of the mind-training slogans. This might sound like an impossible aspiration. As one man said to me, "Always is a very long time." Yet as we train in unblocking our basic goodness, we'll find that every moment contains the free-flowing openness and warmth that characterize unlimited joy.

This is the path we take in cultivating joy: learning not to armor our basic goodness, learning to appreciate what we have. Most of the time we don't do this. Rather than appreciate where we are, we continually struggle and nurture our dissatisfaction. It's like trying to get the flowers to grow by pouring cement on the garden.

But as we use the bodhichitta practices to train, we may come to the point where we see the magic of the present moment; we may gradually wake up to the truth that we have always been warriors living in a sacred world. This is the ongoing experience of limitless joy. We won't always experience this, it's true. But year by year it becomes more and more accessible.

Once a cook at Gampo Abbey was feeling very unhappy. Like most of us, she kept feeding the gloom with her actions and her thoughts; hour by hour her mood was getting darker. She decided to try to ventilate her escalating emotions by baking chocolate chip cookies. Her plan backfired, however—she burned them all to a crisp. At that point, rather than dump the burned cookies in the garbage, she stuffed them into her pockets and backpack and went out for a walk. She trudged along the dirt road, her head hanging down and her mind burning with resentment. She was saying to herself, "So where's all the beauty and magic I keep hearing about?"

At that moment she looked up. There walking toward her was a little fox. Her mind stopped and she held her breath and watched. The fox sat down right in front of her, gazing up expectantly. She reached into her pockets and pulled out some cookies. The fox ate them and slowly trotted away. She told this story to all of us at the abbey, saying: "I learned today that life is very precious. Even when we're determined to block the magic, it will get through and wake us up. That little fox taught me that no matter how shut down we get, we can always look outside our cocoon and connect with joy."

11

Enhancing the Training in Joy

> To make things as easy as possible to understand, we can summarize the four boundless qualities in the single phrase "a kind heart." Just train yourself to have a kind heart always and in all situations.
>
> —PATRUL RINPOCHE

HOW DO WE MAKE THE TEACHINGS REAL? In the midst of our overscheduled lives, how do we discover our inherent clarity and compassion? How do we develop trust that openness and maitri are available even in the most frantic moments? When we feel left out, inadequate, or lonely, can we take a warrior's perspective and contact bodhichitta?

Sharing the heart is a simple practice that can be used at any time and in every situation. It enlarges our view and helps us remember our interconnection. A version of tonglen on the spot, it is also a method for enhancing our ability to rejoice.

The essence of this practice is that when we encounter pain in our life we breathe into our heart with the recognition that others also feel this. It's a way of acknowledging when we are closing down and of training to open up. When we encounter any pleasure or tenderness in our life, we cherish that and rejoice. Then we make the wish that others could also experience this delight or this relief. In a nutshell, when life is pleasant, think of others. When life is a burden, think of others. If this is the only training we ever remember to do, it will benefit us tremendously and everyone else as well. It's a way of bringing whatever we encounter onto the path of awakening bodhichitta.

Even the simplest of things can be the basis of this practice—a beautiful morning, a good meal, a shower. Although there are many such fleeting ordinary moments in our days, we usually speed right past them. We forget what joy they can bring. So the first step is to stop, notice, and appreciate what is happening. Even if this is all we do, it's revolutionary. Then we think of someone who is suffering and wish that the person could have this pleasure to sweeten up his or her life.

When we practice giving in this way, we don't bypass our own pleasure. Say we're eating a delicious strawberry. We don't think, "Oh, I shouldn't be enjoying this so much. Other people don't even have a crust of bread." We just fully appreciate the luscious fruit. Then we wish that Pete or Rita could have such pleasure. We wish that anyone who is suffering could experience such delight.

Discomfort of any kind also becomes the basis for practice. We breathe in knowing that our pain is shared; there are people all over the earth feeling just as we do right now. This simple gesture is a seed of compassion for self and other. If we want, we can go further. We can wish that a specific person or all beings could be free of suffering and its causes. In this way our toothaches, our insomnia, our divorces, and our terror become our link with all humanity.

A woman wrote me about practicing with her daily misery in traffic. Her resentment and her uptightness, the fear of missing an appointment, had become her heart connection with all the other people sitting fuming in their cars. She'd begun to feel her kinship with the people all around her and to even look forward to her daily "traffic jam tonglen."

This simple way of training with pleasure and pain allows us to use what we have, wherever we are, to connect with other people. It engenders on-the-spot bravery, which is what it will take to heal ourselves and our brothers and sisters on the planet.

12

Thinking Bigger

Train without bias in all areas.
It is crucial always to do this pervasively
and wholeheartedly.

—MIND-TRAINING SLOGAN OF ATISHA

BY PRACTICING MAITRI, compassion, and rejoicing, we are training in thinking bigger, in opening up as wholeheartedly as we can to ourselves, to our friends, and even to the people we dislike. We are cultivating the unbiased state of equanimity. Without this fourth boundless quality, the other three are limited by our habit of liking and disliking, accepting and rejecting.

Whenever someone asked a certain Zen master how he was, he would always answer, "I'm okay." Finally one of his students said, "Roshi, how can you always be okay? Don't you ever have a bad day?" The Zen master answered, "Sure I do. On bad days, I'm okay. On good days, I'm also okay." This is equanimity.

The traditional image for equanimity is a banquet

to which everyone is invited. That means that everyone and everything, without exception, is on the guest list. Consider your worst enemy. Consider someone who would do you harm. Consider Pol Pot and Hitler and drug pushers hooking young people. Imagine inviting them to this feast.

Training in equanimity is learning to open the door to all, welcoming all beings, inviting life to come visit. Of course, as certain guests arrive, we'll feel fear and aversion. We allow ourselves to open the door just a crack if that's all that we can presently do, and we allow ourselves to shut the door when necessary. Cultivating equanimity is a work in progress. We aspire to spend our lives training in the loving-kindness and courage that it takes to receive whatever appears—sickness, health, poverty, wealth, sorrow, and joy. We welcome and get to know them all.

Equanimity is bigger than our usual limited perspective. That we hope to get what we want and fear losing what we have—this describes our habitual predicament. The Buddhist teachings identify eight variations on this tendency to hope and fear: pleasure and pain, praise and blame, gain and loss, fame and disgrace. As long as we're caught in one of these extremes, the potential for the other is always there. They just chase each other around. No lasting happiness comes from being caught in this cycle of attraction and aversion. We can never get life to work out so that we eliminate everything we fear and end up with all

the goodies. Therefore the warrior-bodhisattva cultivates equanimity, the vast mind that doesn't narrow
reality into for and against, liking and disliking.

To cultivate equanimity we practice catching ourselves when we feel attraction or aversion, before it
hardens into grasping or negativity. We train in staying
with the soft spot and use our biases as stepping-stones
for connecting with the confusion of others. Strong
emotions are useful in this regard. Whatever arises, no
matter how bad it feels, can be used to extend our
kinship to others who suffer the same kind of aggression or craving—who, just like us, get hooked by hope
and fear. This is how we come to appreciate that everyone's in the same boat. We all desperately need more
insight into what leads to happiness and what leads
to pain.

Recently I was at a practice center visiting a friend.
Over a few days, I heard many people saying how she
was always late for everything. They were feeling in-
convenienced and irritated. She would always justify her
tardiness with what seemed to her good reasons. That
she was even self-righteous got under people's skin.

One day I came upon my friend sitting on a bench.
Her face was red and she was trembling with rage.
She'd had an appointment with someone and she'd
been waiting for fifteen minutes and the person hadn't
shown up.

It was hard not to point out the irony of her reaction. However, I waited to see if she might recognize

that the tables had just been turned, that this was what she'd been putting others through for years. But that insight never came. She couldn't yet put herself in their shoes. Instead she stayed completely indignant, escalating her anger by writing outraged notes. She wasn't yet ready to feel her kinship with all the people she had kept waiting. Just as most of us do, she unwittingly intensified her own suffering. Instead of letting the experience soften her up, she used it to strengthen her hardness and indifference.

It's easy to continue, even after years of practice, to harden into a position of anger and indignation. However, if we can contact the vulnerability and rawness of resentment or rage or whatever it is, a bigger perspective can emerge. In the moment that we choose to abide with the energy instead of acting it out or repressing it, we are training in equanimity, in thinking bigger than right and wrong. This is how all the four limitless qualities evolve from limited to limitless: we practice catching our mind hardening into fixed views and do our best to soften. Through softening, the barriers come down.

An on-the-spot equanimity practice is to walk down the street with the intention of staying as awake as possible to whomever we meet. This is training in being emotionally honest with ourselves and becoming more available to others. As we pass people we simply notice whether we open up or shut down. We notice if we feel attraction, aversion, or indifference, without adding anything extra like self-judgment. We might feel compassion toward someone who looks depressed, or cheered up by someone who's smiling to himself. We might feel fear of and aversion to another person without even knowing why. Noticing where we open up and where we shut down—without praise or blame—is the basis of our practice. Practicing this way for even one block of a city street can be an eye-opener.

We can take the practice even further by using what comes up as the basis for empathy and understanding. Closed feelings like fear or revulsion thus become an opportunity to remember that others also get caught this way. Open states like friendliness and delight also connect us very personally with the people that we pass on the streets. Either way, we are stretching our hearts.

As with the other limitless qualities, equanimity can be practiced formally in seven stages. When we have a feeling of spaciousness and ease that's not caught up in preference or prejudice, this is equanimity. We can wish for ourselves and our loved ones to dwell in that sense of freedom. Then we extend that aspiration to our friend and to neutral persons and to our enemy. We then have the aspiration that all five of us could dwell in equanimity. Finally we can extend the aspiration to all beings in time and space. "May all beings dwell in the great equanimity, free from passion, aggression, and prejudice."

We can also do equanimity practice before beginning the loving-kindness or compassion practices. Simply reflect on how much pain is caused by grasping and aversion, how much pain there is in our fear of losing happiness, how much pain there is in feeling that certain people are not worthy of our compassion or love. Then we can wish for the strength and courage to feel unlimited maitri and unlimited compassion for all beings without exception—including those we dislike and fear. With this intention we begin the seven-step practices.

As the *Maitri Sutra* says, "With a boundless mind one could cherish all living beings, radiating friendliness over the entire world, above, below, and all around without limit." In practicing equanimity, we train in widening our circle of understanding and compassion to include the good and the bad, the beautiful and the ugly. However, limitless equanimity, free of any prejudice at all, is not the same as an ultimate harmony where everything is finally smooth. It is more a matter of being fully engaged with whatever comes to our door. We could call it being completely alive.

Training in equanimity requires that we leave behind some baggage: the comfort of rejecting whole parts of our experience, for example, and the security of welcoming only what is pleasant. The courage to continue with this unfolding process comes from self-compassion and from giving ourselves plenty of time.

If we continue to practice this way over the months and years, we will feel our hearts and minds grow bigger. When people ask me how long this will take, I say, "At least until you die."

13

Meeting the Enemy

With unfailing kindness, your life always presents
what you need to learn. Whether
you stay home or work in an office or whatever,
the next teacher is going to pop right up.

—CHARLOTTE JŌKO BECK

THE ESSENCE OF BRAVERY is being without self-deception. However, it's not so easy to take a
straight look at what we do. Seeing ourselves clearly is
initially uncomfortable and embarrassing. As we train
in clarity and steadfastness, we see things we'd prefer to
deny—judgmentalness, pettiness, arrogance. These are
not sins but temporary and workable habits of mind.
The more we get to know them, the more they lose
their power. This is how we come to trust that our
basic nature is utterly simple, free of struggle between
good and bad.

A warrior begins to take responsibility for the direction of her life. It's as if we are lugging around

unnecessary baggage. Our training encourages us to open the bags and look closely at what we are carrying. In doing this we begin to understand that much of it isn't needed anymore.

There is a traditional teaching that supports us in this process: the near and far enemies of the four limitless qualities. The near enemy is something that's similar to one of these four qualities. Rather than setting us free, however, it burdens us. The far enemy is the quality's opposite; it also gets in our way.

The near enemy or misunderstanding of loving-kindness is attachment. There's a Tibetan word, *lhenchak*, that describes this well. "Lhenchak" points at how free-flowing love can go astray and get stuck. It is taught that the strongest lhenchak occurs in the following three relationships: between parents and children, between lovers, and between spiritual teachers and their students. Lhenchak is characterized by clinging and self-involvement. It's like weaving ourselves into a web of shared neurosis. By its nature, it inhibits human growth. Inevitably the lhenchak relationship turns into a source of irritation and blindness.

Loving-kindness is different from lhenchak. It is not based on need. It is genuine appreciation and care for the well-being of another person, a respect for an individual's value. We can love someone for his own sake, not because he is worthy or unworthy, not because he is loving toward us or he isn't. This goes beyond relationships with people. Loving even a flower without lhenchak, we see it more clearly and feel more tenderness for its inherent perfection.

We get an interesting hit on the emotional roller coaster of lhenchak when we start to move through the seven stages of aspiration. Someone who's theoretically quite dear to us can end up in several categories. In fact, it's frequently not our partners or parents whom we put in the category of unconditionally beloved. They move around day by day, from loved one to difficult person.

The far enemy or opposite of loving-kindness is hatred or aversion. The obvious drawback of aversion is that it isolates us from others. It strengthens the illusion that we are separate. However, right in the tightness and heat of hatred is the soft spot of bodhichitta. It is our vulnerability in difficult encounters that causes us to shut down. When a relationship brings up old memories and ancient discomforts, we become afraid and harden our hearts. Just at the moment when tears could come to our eyes, we pull back and do something mean.

Jarvis Masters, my friend on death row, tells the story of a fellow inmate named Freddie who started to fall apart when he heard of his grandmother's death. He didn't want to let the men around him see him cry and struggled to keep his pain from showing. His friends saw that he was about to explode and reached out to comfort him. Then Freddie started swinging violently. The tower guards began to shoot and yell for

Freddie's friends to back away. But they wouldn't. They knew they had to calm him down. They screamed at the guards that there was something wrong with him, that he needed help. They grabbed Freddie and held him down, and every one of them was crying. As Jarvis put it, they reached out to Freddie, "not as hardened prisoners, but simply as human beings."

There are three near enemies of compassion: pity, overwhelm, and idiot compassion. Pity or professional warmth is easily mistaken for true compassion. When we identify ourselves as the helper, it means we see others as helpless. Instead of feeling the pain of the other person, we set ourselves apart. If we've ever been on the receiving end of pity we know how painful it feels. Instead of warmth and support all we feel is distance. With true compassion these up-down identities are stripped away.

Overwhelm is a sense of helplessness. We feel that there is so much suffering—whatever we do is to no avail. We've become discouraged. There are two ways I've found effective in working with overwhelm. One is to train with a less challenging subject, to find a situation we feel that we can handle.

A woman wrote to me that when she read about these compassion practices she felt inspired to do them for her son, who is addicted to heroin. She naturally longed for him to be free of his suffering and its causes. She naturally wanted him to have happiness and relief. But when she started to practice she found that she couldn't do it. As soon as she would get in touch with the truth of his situation, it overwhelmed her. She decided instead to do tonglen and the aspirations for the families of all the young people addicted to heroin. She tried, and she couldn't do that either. The situation was too frightening and too raw.

Around that time she turned on the television and there was her hometown football team who had just lost a game. She could see the heartbreak in their faces. So she started doing tonglen and compassionate aspirations for the losing team. She was able to contact her genuine empathy without overwhelm. When doing the practices became possible, her fears and her sense of helplessness decreased. Gradually she was able to make the stretch into practicing for the other families and finally for her son.

So starting with something workable can be powerful magic. When we find the place where our heart can stay engaged, the compassion begins to spread by itself.

The second way of training with overwhelm is to keep our attention on the other person. This one takes more courage. When someone else's pain triggers fear in us, we turn inward and start erecting walls. We panic because we feel we can't handle the pain. Sometimes we should trust this panic as a sign that we aren't yet ready to open so far. But sometimes instead of closing down or resisting we might have the courage to do something unpredictable: turn our attention back toward the other person. This is the same as keeping our heart open to the pain. If we can't shift our attention, perhaps we can let the story line go and feel the energy of the pain in our body for one second without freaking out or retreating. However, if none of these is yet possible, we engender some compassion for our current limitations and go forward.

The third near enemy of compassion is idiot compassion. This is when we avoid conflict and protect our good image by being kind when we should say a definite "no." Compassion doesn't imply only trying to be good. When we find ourselves in an aggressive relationship, we need to set clear boundaries. The kindest thing we can do for everyone concerned is to know when to say "enough." Many people use Buddhist ideals to justify self-debasement. In the name of not shutting our heart, we let people walk all over us. It is said that in order not to break our vow of compassion we have to learn when to stop aggression and draw the line. There are times when the only way to bring down the barriers is to set boundaries.

The far enemy or opposite of compassion is cruelty. When we reach the limit of how much suffering we can take, we sometimes use cruelty as a defense against our fear of pain. This is common for anyone who was abused as a child. Instead of feeling kindness for those who are defenseless and weak, we can feel an irrational desire to hurt them. We protect our vulnerability and fear by hardening. If we do not recognize that by doing this we hurt ourselves as much as we hurt others, we'll never get free. Booker T. Washington was right when he said, "Let no man pull you so low as to make you hate him." Cruelty when rationalized or unacknowledged destroys us.

The near enemy of joyfulness is overexcitement. We can churn ourselves into a manic state and mistake riding high above the sorrows of the world for unconditional joy. Again, instead of connecting us with others, this separates us. Authentic joy is not a euphoric state or a feeling of being high. Rather, it is a state of appreciation that allows us to participate fully in our lives. We train in rejoicing in the good fortune of self and others.

The far enemy of joy is envy. Until I started working with the practice of rejoicing in the good fortune of others, I never realized I could be so envious. To say that this was humbling is an understatement. I was amazed to see how frequently I react to others' success with resentment. When I heard that my acquaintance's book had sold more copies than mine, I instantly felt envious. Maybe it's because these practices expose our hidden faults that we are sometimes reluctant to do them. But that's one reason we continue to train: it takes practice to stick with ourselves as we are, in our totality.

The near enemy of equanimity is detachment or indifference. Especially in spiritual practice, it is easy to mistake dangling above the unkemptness of life for genuine equanimity. We are open and friendly and serene and proud that we've transcended emotional upheaval. If we feel distress, embarrassment, or anger, we think we've really blown it. Yet feeling emotional upheaval is not a spiritual faux pas; it's the place where the warrior learns compassion. It's where we learn to stop struggling with ourselves. It's only when we can dwell in these places that scare us that equanimity becomes unshakable.

The far enemy of equanimity is prejudice. We get self-righteous about our beliefs and set ourselves solidly for or against others. We take sides. We become closed-minded. We have enemies. This polarization is an obstacle to the genuine equanimity that informs compassionate action. If we wish to alleviate injustice and suffering, we have to do it with an unprejudiced mind.

The heart practices set us up to become intimately acquainted with the near and far enemies. Our training is almost like inviting them to visit. As we move closer to our genuine ability to rejoice, we get to know our jealousy and resentment. As we start training in opening our hearts, we get a close look at prejudice and indifference. When we go through the stages of aspiration, these closed-down feelings become more vivid.

These enemies are good teachers that show us that we can accept ourselves and others complete with imperfections. We develop trust in our open and forgiving mind. In doing so, we discover the strength that allows us to enter into the suffering of the world.

14

Fresh Start

We are all children of the Great Spirit,
we all belong to Mother Earth. Our planet
is in great trouble and if we keep carrying
old grudges and do not work together,
we will all die.

—CHIEF SEATTLE

FORGIVENESS IS an essential ingredient of bodhi-chitta practice. It allows us to let go of the past and make a fresh start.

When a close friend of mine was dying, a Tibetan teacher told her to review her life with honesty and compassion. This process led her to some pretty dark places, corners of her mind where she was stuck in guilt and resentment. The teacher then instructed her in forgiveness, saying that the most important thing to do was to forgive herself. He suggested that she do a variation on tonglen. She should begin by visualizing herself and then intentionally bring up all her life's regrets. The point was not to dwell in painful memories but to contact the feelings underlying the pain: guilt or shame, confusion or remorse. The feelings didn't have to be named; she was to contact the stuckness in a nonverbal way.

The next step was to breathe these feelings into her heart, opening it as wide as she possibly could, and then to send herself forgiveness. After that, she was to think of others feeling the same anguish and to breathe their pain and hers into her heart and to send everyone forgiveness. My friend found this to be a healing process. It allowed her to make amends with those she had hurt and those who had hurt her. She was able to let go of her shame and anger before she died.

A woman who came to Gampo Abbey for a tonglen retreat had suffered severe sexual abuse from her father. She strongly identified with caged birds; she told me that she often felt like a bird in a cage. During tonglen, she would breathe in the feeling of being small and caged; on the outbreath she would open the door and let all the birds out. One day as she was sending and taking in this way, she experienced one of the birds flying out and landing on a man's shoulder. Then the man turned around and she saw it was her father. For the first time in her life she was able to forgive him.

Forgiveness, it seems, cannot be forced. When we are brave enough to open our hearts to ourselves, however, forgiveness will emerge.

There is a simple practice we can do to cultivate forgiveness. First we acknowledge what we feel—shame, revenge, embarrassment, remorse. Then we forgive ourselves for being human. Then, in the spirit of not wallowing in the pain, we let go and make a fresh start. We don't have to carry the burden with us anymore. We can acknowledge, forgive, and start anew. If we practice this way, little by little we'll learn to abide with the feeling of regret for having hurt ourselves and others. We will also learn self-forgiveness. Eventually, at our own speed, we'll even find our capacity to forgive those who have done us harm. We will discover forgiveness as a natural expression of the open heart, an expression of our basic goodness. This potential is inherent in every moment. Each moment is an opportunity to make a fresh start.

15

Strength

Practice the five strengths,
The condensed heart instructions.

— MIND-TRAINING SLOGAN OF ATISHA

THE FIVE STRENGTHS are *strong determination, familiarization* with the bodhichitta teachings and practices, *the seed of goodness* that is found in every living being, the practice of *reproach*, and the power of *aspiration*. These are five ways that a warrior increases confidence and inspiration.

Strong determination is our commitment to use our lives to dissolve the indifference, aggression, and grasping that separate us from one another. It is a commitment to respect whatever life brings. As warriors-in-training we develop wholehearted determination to use discomfort as an opportunity for awakening, rather than trying to make it disappear. How do we abide with disagreeable emotions without retreating into our familiar strategies? How do we catch our thoughts before they become 100 percent believable and solidify into "us" against "them"? Where do we find the warmth that is essential to the transformative process? We are committed to exploring these questions. We are determined to find a way to realize our kinship with others, determined to keep training in opening our mind. This strong determination generates strength.

Familiarization is the strength that comes to us when we take the teachings to heart, becoming familiar with them by using them over and over. When we wake up in the morning and start our bodhichitta training anew, what will we use as material? Just our usual day in all its variations—pleasant, unpleasant, or simply mundane.

What will happen to us today is completely unknown, as unknown as what will happen at death. Whatever happens, our commitment is to use it to awaken our heart. As one of the slogans says, "All activities should be done with one intention." That intention is to realize our connection with all beings.

Recently I had the pleasure of going to a friend's swimming pool in the country. I had just received a letter, so when I got there I sat in the car and read it. The letter was very straightforward. It pointed out to me that in a particular situation I had neglected to communicate with the right people. My lack of clear communication had caused confusion and disappointment. Reading this letter brought up a surprising amount of pain. Everything in me wanted to exit, and

I adopted a common strategy: blame. It was someone else's fault that this had happened.

Right there in the car, I got out a pen and began to write a letter to the person I was blaming. I made the blame solid and real: I put it down on paper. I knew enough to stop writing, but I said to myself, "How can I be asking other people to do this kind of practice? It's asking too much. It's too challenging, too hard." I got out of the car and sat down next to the pool and the pain was so consuming that at first I forgot all about the bodhichitta teachings. I didn't want to be a warrior. On the other hand, I know that unhappiness lies with exiting, with pointing myself away from the discomfort. Believe me, I've done it enough to know that this is true.

I tried to encourage myself along the line that I am bigger than my thoughts and emotions. I also acknowledged my thoughts, listening to what I was saying about myself and others. But no shift was happening, absolutely none.

Finally I got into the pool and started to swim laps. After going back and forth about six times, I put my elbows on the side of the pool and began to weep. At that point I was overwhelmed by a sense of how we suffer.

Then, not because I was doing a particular practice but because I'm so familiar with finding the soft spot, a reservoir of empathy arose seemingly out of nowhere, completely available to me. I was able to connect profoundly with my brothers and sisters all over the world.

All I had done there sitting by the pool was somehow to stay. I was trying to recall the teaching and to practice, but it didn't really matter what I did. There is not a formula for doing this kind of work. My willingness to stay with the discomfort was what allowed something to shift. Then the reservoir of compassion began to emerge.

Frequently there is no such reward. Staying with sorrow or pain is not necessarily an immediately gratifying process. But over time, we begin to feel lighter and more courageous. Familiarization with the teachings and the bodhichitta practices in an ongoing way is how we learn to reside with distress and to experience our shared humanity. This is how we make the teachings useful and heartfelt in our lives.

The third source of inspiration is the *seed of goodness*. That reservoirs of openness and tenderness are available to us is the strength of the positive seed, the seed of bodhichitta. Sometimes remembering our basic goodness takes a leap of faith. The trick is to connect with the soft spot that we already have. Sometimes it helps to find little ways that the seed of goodness manifests in our life. To find our ability to rejoice and to care, even when it's fleeting, strengthens our confidence. To see how we block our hearts and close our minds brings self-compassion and the longing not to do that anymore.

So our practice is to keep watering the seed. We water it by thinking of others, both when we're happy and when we're in distress. We water it by recognizing our kinship with all beings throughout time and space. We water it by noticing our negative and positive reactions to whomever and whatever we meet. We water it with gentleness and honesty. We learn to ask, "How can I use this suffering and this joy as a vehicle for transformation?" And we practice being kind when we get stuck.

The fourth strength is *reproach*. Reproach can be tricky because it backfires if there's no maitri. Its strength is that if used with loving-kindness it will steer us away from debilitating habitual patterns. The gentlest method of reproach is to ask ourselves, "Have I ever done this before?" When we suspect that we're turning away from the moment, we can say to ourselves as a reminder, "Does this way of acting or thinking feel familiar?"

Trungpa Rinpoche encouraged his students to be eccentric bodhisattvas and to give ego a hard time. He suggested that instead of listening to the radio or singing in the shower, we talk to our ego. "Okay, ego, you've been giving me problems for my entire life and now I'm getting a whole lot smarter. I'm not going to be under your sway for one more day!"

Patrul Rinpoche tells some wonderful stories about a monk called Geshe Ben. Reproaching the ego was one of his main practices. He specialized in catching himself getting hooked. One day some patrons invited

Geshe Ben for a meal. After it was over, he was left alone in the room with a big bag of flour. Without thinking, he put his cup in the bag and started to take some for his journey. With his hand in the bag he exclaimed, "Ben, look what you're doing!" Then he shouted, "Thief! Thief!" The patrons rushed in to find him standing there, his hand still in the flour, yelling, "I've caught him! I've caught him! I've caught the thief red-handed!" That's the spirit of reproach. Including a sense of humor is what allows it to work.

The next time Geshe Ben had a meal with his patrons, they were serving other monks as well. Many delicious foods were offered, including yogurt—his favorite—and Ben was at the end of the row. After a while he began to feel nervous that there wouldn't be enough. As the servers ladled the yogurt out, he nervously watched to see how much others were taking, feeling irritated with those who took more and happy with those who took less. Then suddenly he caught himself in the act, shouting, "Ben, look what you're doing!" When finally the servers reached him he covered his bowl saying, "No! No! No more yogurt for this yogurt addict!"

The point of reproach is to develop enough self-respect that when we catch ourselves getting hooked in familiar ways we can stop. We aren't disciplining our badness; we're simply getting smart about what brings suffering and what brings happiness. We're finally giving ourselves a break.

The fifth strength is the strength that comes from *aspiration*. We may not yet feel ready to act, but even in very difficult situations, we can do something to help. We can aspire to arouse bodhichitta, to free ourselves from neurosis and be of benefit. We can aspire to find the warrior's strength and ability to love.

A student told me that early one morning he heard a woman screaming on the street. He was living in an urban practice center; other people woke up and they all went to her aid. But before that happened, when he first heard her screams, he had to acknowledge that he felt aversion toward the woman. He was unprepared even to make the aspiration to be in her shoes. He couldn't aspire to feel her pain. It was too terrifying to imagine being so vulnerable and unprotected. He felt, "Better her than me." So right there, on the spot, he thought of everyone like him who wishes to help but can't. And he made the genuine aspiration that in this very lifetime, he and all the others could work with their fear and remove the barriers of separation.

So these are the five strengths we can utilize in our practice of awakening bodhichitta:

Cultivating *strong determination* and commitment to relate openly with whatever life presents, including our emotional distress.

Building *familiarization* with the bodhichitta practices by utilizing them in formal practice and on the spot.

Watering the *seed of bodhichitta* in both delightful

and miserable situations so that our confidence in this positive seed can grow.

Using *reproach*—with kindness and humor—as a way of catching ourselves before we cause harm to self or other.

Nurturing the habit of *aspiration* for all of us that suffering and its seeds diminish and that wisdom and compassion increase, nurturing the habit of always cultivating our kind heart and open mind.

16

Three Kinds of Laziness

In the garden of gentle sanity
May you be bombarded by coconuts
    of wakefulness.

— CHÖGYAM TRUNGPA RINPOCHE

Laziness is a common human trait. Unfortunately, it inhibits wakeful energy and undermines our confidence and strength. There are three kinds of laziness—comfort orientation, loss of heart, and "couldn't care less." These are three ways that we become stuck in debilitating habitual patterns. Exploring them with curiosity, however, dissolves their power.

The first kind of laziness, comfort orientation, is based on our tendency to avoid inconvenience. We want to take a rest, to give ourselves a break. But soothing ourselves, lulling ourselves, becomes a habit and we become jaded and lazy. If it's raining we drive half a block rather than get wet. At the first hint of heat, we turn on the air conditioner. At the first threat of cold, we turn up the heat. In this way we lose touch with the texture of life. We trust the quick "upper" and become accustomed to automatic results.

This particular brand of laziness can make us aggressive. We become outraged at inconvenience. When the car doesn't work, when we lose our water or electric service, when we have to sit on the cold ground without padding, we explode. Comfort orientation dulls our appreciation of smells and sights and sounds. It also makes us dissatisfied. Somehow we always know in our hearts that pure pleasure is not the route to lasting happiness.

The second kind of laziness is loss of heart. We feel a sense of hopelessness, of "poor me." We feel so poverty-stricken that we aren't up to dealing with the world. We sit in front of the television eating, drinking, and smoking, mindlessly watching show after show. We can't bring ourselves to do anything to ventilate our loss of heart. Even if we manage to crank ourselves up and open the window, we do it with a sense of shame. We make an outer gesture of breaking through laziness, but still hold that essence of hopelessness inside. That gesture of cranking up or pushing through is still an expression of loss of heart. We are still saying to ourselves, "I'm the worst. There's no hope for me. I'll never get it right." Thus we don't really give ourselves a break. We've forgotten how to help ourselves; we lack insight into what would bring us true relief.

The third kind of laziness, "couldn't care less," is

characterized by resentment. We are giving the world the finger. It's similar to loss of heart but much harder. Loss of heart has some kind of softness and vulnerability. Couldn't care less is more aggressive and defiant. "The world is messed up. It's not giving me what I deserve. So why bother?" We go to the bar and drink all day long, and if someone talks to us we pick a fight. Or we shut the curtains, get into bed, and pull the blankets over our heads. If someone tries to cheer us up, heaven help him! We wallow in feeling undervalued and put down. We don't want to find any outlet. We just want to sit around, feeling weighted down with gloom. We use laziness as our way of getting revenge. This kind of laziness can easily turn into incapacitating depression.

There are three habitual methods that human beings use for relating to laziness or any troubling emotion. I call these the three futile strategies—the strategies of attacking, indulging, and ignoring.

The futile strategy of attacking is particularly popular. When we see our laziness we condemn ourselves. We criticize and shame ourselves for indulging in comfort or pitying ourselves or not getting out of bed. We wallow in the feeling of badness and guilt.

The futile strategy of indulging is equally common. We justify and even applaud our laziness. "This is just the way I am. I don't deserve discomfort or inconvenience. I have plenty of reasons to be angry or to sleep twenty-four hours a day." We may be haunted by self-doubt and feelings of inadequacy, but we talk ourselves into condoning our behavior.

The strategy of ignoring is quite effective, at least for a while. We dissociate, space out, go numb. We do anything possible to distance ourselves from the naked truth of our habits. We go on automatic pilot and just avoid looking too closely at what we're doing.

The mind-training practices of the warrior present a fourth alternative, the alternative of an enlightened strategy. This is the strategy of fully experiencing whatever we've been resisting—without exiting in our three habitual ways. We become inquisitive about the three kinds of laziness. With bodhichitta training, we practice not resisting the resistance, touching in with the fundamental tenderness and groundlessness of our being before it hardens. We do this with the clear intention that our ego-clinging diminish and our wisdom and compassion increase.

It's important to recognize that we don't usually want to investigate laziness or any other habit. We want to indulge or ignore or condemn. We want to continue with the three futile strategies because we associate them with relief. We want to continue to escape into comfort orientation, to talk to ourselves endlessly about our loss of heart, or to chew on the fatalism of couldn't care less.

At some point, however, we might begin to get curious and start to ask questions like "Why am I suffering? Why does nothing lighten up? Why do my dissatisfaction and boredom get stronger year by year?"

That's when we might remember our training. That's when we just might feel ready to start experimenting with the warrior's compassionate approach. That's when the instruction to stay with the tenderness and not harden might start to make sense.

So we begin to look into our laziness and experience its quality directly. We come to know our fear of inconvenience, our shame, our resentment, our dullness, and we come to understand that others also feel this way. We pay attention to the stories we tell ourselves and notice how they cause our bodies to tighten. With ongoing practice we understand that we don't have to believe these stories anymore. We do tonglen, sitting meditation, and the other bodhichitta practices as ways of opening to the rawness of emotional energy. We begin to feel some tenderness, realizing that everyone gets caught up as we do and that all of us could be free.

Laziness is not particularly terrible or wonderful. Rather it has a basic living quality that deserves to be experienced just as it is. Perhaps we'll find an irritating, pulsating quality in laziness. We might feel it as dull and heavy or as vulnerable and raw. Whatever we discover, as we explore it further, we find nothing to hold on to, nothing solid, only groundless, wakeful energy.

This process of experiencing laziness directly and nonverbally is transformative. It unlocks a tremendous energy that is usually blocked by our habit of running away. This is because when we stop resisting laziness, our identity as the one who is lazy begins to fall apart completely. Without the blinders of ego, we connect with a fresh outlook, a greater vision. This is how laziness—or any other demon—introduces us to the compassionate life.

17

Bodhisattva Activity

As the buddhas of old gave birth to bodhichitta
And progressively established themselves
   in the training of a bodhisattva,
So I too, for the benefit of beings, give birth
   to bodhichitta
And progressively train myself in that discipline.

—SHANTIDEVA

F EW OF US ARE SATISFIED with retreating from
the world and just working on ourselves. We want
our training to manifest and to be of benefit. The bo-
dhisattva-warrior, therefore, makes a vow to wake up
not just for himself but for the welfare of all beings.

There are six traditional activities in which the bodhisattva trains, six ways of compassionate living:
generosity, discipline, patience, enthusiasm, meditation, and prajna—unconditional wisdom. Traditionally these are called the six paramitas, a Sanskrit word
meaning "gone to the other shore." Each one is an activity we can use to take us beyond aversion and attachment, beyond being all caught up in ourselves, beyond

the illusion of separateness. Each paramita has the ability to take us beyond our fear of letting go.

Through paramita training we learn to be comfortable with uncertainty. Going to the other shore has a groundless quality, a sense of being caught in the middle, being caught in an in-between state. We get into a raft on this shore, where we're struggling with notions of right and wrong, busy solidifying the illusion of ground by constantly seeking predictability. And we're traveling across the river to the other side, where we are liberated from the narrow-mindedness and dualistic thinking that characterize ego-clinging. That's the traditional image.

This is the picture I prefer: In the middle of the river, with the shoreline out of view, the raft begins to disintegrate. We find ourselves with absolutely nothing to hold on to. From our conventional standpoint, this is scary and dangerous. However, one small shift of perspective will tell us that having nothing to hold on to is liberating. We could have faith that we won't drown. Holding on to nothing means we can relax with this fluid, dynamic world.

The prajnaparamita is the key to this training. Without prajnaparamita—or unconditional bodhichitta—the other five activities can be used to give us the illusion of ground. The foundation of the prajnaparamita is mindfulness, an open-ended inquiry into our experience. We question without the intention of finding permanent solutions. We cultivate a mind that is ready and inquisitive, not satisfied with limited or biased views.

It's like lying in bed before dawn and hearing rain on the roof. This simple sound can be disappointing because we were planning a picnic. It can be pleasing because our garden is so dry. But the flexible mind of prajna doesn't draw conclusions of good or bad. It perceives the sound without adding anything extra, without judgments of happy or sad.

It is with this unfixated mind of prajna that we practice generosity, discipline, enthusiasm, patience, and meditation, moving from narrow-mindedness to flexibility and fearlessness.

The essence of generosity is letting go. Pain is always a sign that we are holding on to something—usually ourselves. When we feel unhappy, when we feel inadequate, we get stingy; we hold on tight. Generosity is an activity that loosens us up. By offering whatever we can—a dollar, a flower, a word of encouragement—we are training in letting go. As Suzuki Roshi put it: "To give is nonattachment, just not to attach to anything is to give."

There are so many ways to practice generosity. The main point isn't so much what we give but that we unlock our habit of clinging. A traditional practice is simply to offer an object that we cherish from one hand to the other. A woman I know decided that whatever she was attached to she'd give away. One man gave money to people begging in the streets every day for six months after the death of his father. It was his way of working with grief. Another woman trained in visualizing giving away whatever she most feared losing.

A young couple decided to deal with their ambivalence about panhandlers by giving money to the first person who asked each day. They were sincerely attempting to work with their confusion around the issue of homelessness, but they had an agenda: they would be good, generous people and do their noble deed and then forget about their conflicted feelings for the rest of the day.

One morning a drunk asked the woman for money as she went into a store. Even though he was the first panhandler of the day, his presence disgusted her and she didn't want to give him anything. When she came out of the store she hastily gave him a bill and rushed away. Walking to her car, she heard a voice calling, "Ma'am, ma'am!" She turned and there was the drunk, who said, "I think you made a mistake! You gave me a five."

Giving practice shows us where we're holding back, where we're still clinging. We start with our well-laid plans, but life blows them apart. From a gesture of generosity, true letting go will evolve. Our conventional perspective will begin to change.

It is easy to regard the paramitas as a rigid code of ethics, a list of rules. But the bodhisattva's world is not that simple. The power of the paramitas is not that they are commandments but that they challenge our habitual reactions. This is especially true of the discipline paramita. Discipline is the conduct that de-escalates suffering. The warrior refrains from nonvirtuous actions such as killing, harmful speech, stealing, and sexual misconduct. But these guidelines are not written in stone. The intention to open the heart and mind is what's essential. If we do good deeds with an attitude of superiority or outrage, we simply add more aggression to the planet.

Paramita training has a way of humbling us and keeping us honest. When we practice generosity we become intimate with our grasping. When we practice the discipline of not causing harm we see our rigidity and self-righteousness. Our practice is to work with guidelines of compassionate conduct with the flexible mind of prajna—seeing things without "shoulds" or "should nots."

We aren't drawing upon a code of conduct and condemning everyone who doesn't comply. If we draw a line down the center of a room and tell those in it to put themselves in the category of "virtuous" or "nonvirtuous," are we truly more liberated because we choose "virtuous"? More likely we're just more arrogant and proud. Bodhisattvas are to be found among thieves and prostitutes and murderers.

There is a traditional Buddhist story about a ship captain, Compassionate Heart, who was traveling with five hundred people when a pirate, Angry Spearman, boarded the boat and threatened to kill them all. The captain realized that if the pirate did this, he would be sowing the seeds of his own intense suffering. Moved by compassion for both the pirate and the people, the captain killed Angry Spearman. In the same vein, we sometimes have to tell a lie in order to protect someone from harm.

There is no act that is inherently virtuous or nonvirtuous. The warrior trains in the discipline of not causing harm, knowing that the way to do this skillfully will change with the circumstances. When we practice discipline with flexibility, we become less moralistic and more tolerant.

As we train in the patience paramita, we are first of all patient with ourselves. We learn to relax with the restlessness of our energy—the energy of anger, boredom, and excitement. Patience takes courage. It is not an ideal state of calm. In fact, when we practice patience we will see our agitation far more clearly.

One man decided to train in patience on his morning commute. He thought he was succeeding beautifully. He was patient when people cut in front of him. He was patient when they honked their horns. When he became anxious that the heavy traffic was going to make him late, he was able to relax with his agitated energy. He was doing great. Then he had to stop for a woman in a crosswalk. She was walking very slowly. The man sat there practicing patience—letting the thoughts go and connecting with his restlessness as directly as he could. Suddenly the woman turned, kicked his car, and started screaming at him. At that point he totally lost his calm and started screaming back. Then he remembered hearing that in practicing patience we see our anger far more clearly. He started breathing in for the woman and for himself. Here they were—two strangers screaming at each other—and he felt the absurdity and tenderness of their situation.

Being ambitious about paramita practice is a setup for failure. When we give up the hope of doing it right and the fear of getting it wrong, we realize that winning and losing are both acceptable. In either case, we have nothing to hang on to. Moment by moment we are traveling to the other shore.

The paramita of enthusiasm is connected with joy. In practicing this paramita, like little children learning to walk, we train with eagerness but without a goal. This joyful, uplifted energy isn't a matter of luck. It takes ongoing training in mindfulness and maitri, in dissolving the barriers and opening the heart. As we learn to relax with groundlessness, this enthusiasm will emerge. We practice what is called the threefold purity—no big deal about the doer, no big deal about the action, no big deal about the result. This joyful exertion is rooted in no expectation, no ambition, no hope of fruition. We just eagerly put one foot in front of the other and are not discouraged when we fall flat on our faces. We act without self-congratulation or self-censure, without fearing criticism or expecting applause.

Through continual practice we find out how to cross over the boundary between stuckness and waking up. It depends on our willingness to experience directly feelings we've been avoiding for many years. This willingness to stay open to what scares us weakens our habits of avoidance. It's the way that ego-clinging becomes ventilated and begins to fade.

The threefold purity is also the essence of the meditation paramita. When we sit down to meditate we leave behind the idea of the perfect meditator, the ideal meditation, and preconceived results. We train in simply being present. We open ourselves completely to the pain and the pleasure of our life. We train in precision, gentleness, and letting go. Because we see our thoughts and emotions with compassion, we stop struggling against ourselves. We learn to recognize when we're all caught up and to trust that we can let go. Thus the blockages created by our habits and prejudices start falling apart. In this way, the wisdom we were blocking—the wisdom of bodhichitta—becomes available.

So these are the six activities of the warrior:

Generosity. Giving as a path of learning to let go.

Discipline. Training in not causing harm in a way that is daring and flexible.

Patience. Training in abiding with the restlessness of our energy and letting things evolve at their own speed. If waking up takes forever, still we go moment by moment, giving up all hope of fruition and enjoying the process.

Joyful enthusiasm. Letting go of our perfectionism and connecting with the living quality of every moment.

Meditation. Training in coming back to being right here with gentleness and precision.

Prajna. Cultivating an open, inquiring mind.

With these six activities of the bodhisattva, we learn how to travel to the other shore, and we do our best to take everyone we can find along with us.

18

Groundlessness

> The everyday practice is simply to develop
> a complete acceptance and openness to all
> situations and emotions, and to all people,
> experiencing everything totally without mental
> reservations and blockages, so that one never
> withdraws or centralizes into oneself.
>
> —DILGO KHYENTSE RINPOCHE

A T ONE TIME the Buddha gathered his students together at a spot called Vulture Peak Mountain. Here he presented some revolutionary teachings— teachings on the wide-open, groundless dimension of our being—known traditionally as shunyata, as unconditional bodhichitta, as prajnaparamita.

The Buddha had already been teaching on ground- lessness for some time. Many of the students there on Vulture Peak Mountain had a profound realization of impermanence and egolessness, the truth that nothing—including ourselves—is solid or predictable. They understood the suffering that results from grasping and fixation. They had learned this from Buddha himself; they had experienced its profundity in meditation. But the Buddha knew that our tendency to seek solid ground is deeply rooted. Ego can use anything to maintain the illusion of security, including the belief in insubstantiality and change.

So the Buddha did something shocking. With the prajnaparamita teachings he pulled the rug out completely, taking his students further into groundlessness. He told the audience that whatever they believed had to be let go, that dwelling upon any description of reality was a trap. This was not comfortable news for the audience to hear.

It reminds me of the story of Krishnamurti, who was raised to be the avatar by the Theosophists. His elders continually told the other students that when the avatar manifested fully, his teachings would be electrifying and revolutionary, shaking up the very foundations of their beliefs. This turned out to be true, but not quite in the way they had imagined. When Krishnamurti finally became head of the Order of the Star, he called the whole society together and officially disbanded it, saying that it was harmful because it gave them too much ground.

The Vulture Peak experience was something like that for the Buddha's students. It wiped away all their existing conceptions about the nature of reality. The Buddha's principal message that day was that holding on to *anything* blocks wisdom. *Any* conclusions we might draw must be let go. The only way to fully understand the bodhichitta teachings, the only way to practice them fully, is to abide in the unconditional openness of the prajnaparamita, patiently cutting through all our tendencies to hang on.

During this teaching, known as *The Heart Sutra,* the Buddha actually didn't say a word. He went into a state of deep meditation and let the bodhisattva of compassion, Avalokiteshvara, do the talking. This courageous warrior, also known as Kuan-yin, expressed his experience of the prajnaparamita on behalf of the Buddha. His insight was not based on intellect but came through his practice. He saw clearly that everything is empty. Then one of the principal disciples of the Buddha, a monk named Shariputra, began to question Avalokiteshvara. This is an important point. Even though a great bodhisattva was teaching and the Buddha was clearly in charge, the profound meaning emerged only through questioning. Nothing was taken complacently or on blind faith.

Shariputra is a role model for us as students. He wasn't willing just to accept what he heard; he wanted to know for himself what was true. So he asked Avalokiteshvara, "In all the words and actions and thoughts of my life, how do I apply the prajnaparamita? What is the key to training in this practice? What view do I take?"

Avalokiteshvara answered with the most famous of Buddhist paradoxes: "Form is emptiness, emptiness also is form. Emptiness is no other than form, form is no other than emptiness." When I first heard this, I had no idea whatsoever what he was talking about. My mind went completely blank. His explanation, like the prajnaparamita itself, is inexpressible, indescribable, inconceivable. Form is that which simply *is* before we project our beliefs onto it. The prajnaparamita represents a completely fresh take, an unfettered mind where anything is possible.

Prajna is the unfiltered expression of the open ear, open eye, open mind that is found in every living being. Thich Nhat Hanh translates the word as "understanding." It's a fluid process, not something definite and concrete that can be summed up or measured.

This prajnaparamita, this inexpressibility, is our human experience. It is not particularly regarded as a peaceful state of mind or as a disturbed one. It is a state of basic intelligence that is open, questioning, and unbiased. Whether it comes in the form of curiosity, bewilderment, shock, or relaxation isn't really the issue. We train when we're caught off guard and when our life is up in the air.

We train, as Trungpa Rinpoche said, in "not afraid to be a fool." We cultivate a simple, direct relationship with our being—no philosophizing, no moralizing, no judgments. Whatever arises in our mind is workable.

So when Avalokiteshvara says, "Form is emptiness," he's referring to this simple, direct relationship with the immediacy of experience—direct contact with blood and sweat and flowers, with love as well as hate. First we wipe away our preconceptions and then we even have to let go of our belief that we should look at things without preconceptions. We keep pulling out our own rug. When we perceive form as empty, without any barriers or veils, we understand the perfection of things just as they are. One could become addicted to this experience. It could give us a sense of freedom from the dubiousness of our emotions and the illusion that we could dangle above the messiness of our lives.

But "emptiness also is form" turns the tables. Emptiness continually manifests as war and peace, as grief, as birth, old age, sickness, and death, as well as joy. We are challenged to stay in touch with the heart-throbbing quality of being alive. That's why we train in the relative bodhichitta practices of the four limitless ones and tonglen. They help us to engage fully in the vividness of life with an open, unclouded mind. Things are as bad and as good as they seem. There's no need to add anything extra.

Imagine a dialogue with the Buddha. He asks, "How do you perceive reality?" and we answer honestly and say, "I perceive it as separate from me, and solid." He says, "No, look deeper."

So we go away and meditate and sincerely contemplate this question. We return to the Buddha and say, "I know the answer now. The answer is that everything is not solid, everything is empty." And he says, "No. Look deeper." We say, "Well, that's impossible. It's either one way or the other: empty or not empty, right?" and he says, "No." If this were our boss, perhaps we wouldn't care, but this is the Buddha, so we think, "Maybe I have to hang in here a bit and go further with the irritation I'm feeling at not being given any satisfaction."

So we meditate and contemplate this question; we discuss it with our friends. Next time we see the Buddha we say, "I think I can answer your question. Everything is both empty and not empty simultaneously." And he says, "No." Believe me, we're feeling very groundless and that means rattled. It's uncomfortable not to be able to get ground under our feet. But the process here is of unmasking: even though we're irritated and anxious, we're moving closer to seeing the true, unfixed nature of mind. Since "no" is all we can get out of the Buddha, we go home and spend the next year trying to answer this riddle. It's like a Zen koan.

Eventually, we return and say, "Okay. There's only one other possible answer. The nature of reality is that it neither exists nor doesn't exist. It is neither form nor emptiness." And we feel good! It's a beautiful groundless answer. But the Buddha says, "No, that's too limited an understanding." Maybe at this point his "no" is such a shock that we experience the wide-open mind of prajnaparamita, the mind that is satisfied with no resting place at all.

After Avalokiteshvara told Shariputra that "form is emptiness; emptiness also is form," he went even further, pointing out that there is nothing—not even the Buddha's teachings—to hold on to: no three marks of existence, no suffering, no end of suffering, no imprisonment, no liberation. The story goes that many of the students were so dumbfounded by these teachings that they had heart attacks. A Tibetan teacher suggested that more likely they just got up and walked out of the talk. Like the Theosophists with Krishnamurti, they didn't want to hear this. Just like us. We don't like to have our basic assumptions challenged. It's too threatening.

Now, if this teaching had come only from Avalokiteshvara, the students might have been able to rationalize their fears. "This is just a warrior on the path, not so different from us. He's very wise and compassionate, of course, but he has been known to get things wrong." But the Buddha was sitting right there in deep meditation, clearly pleased with this presentation of how to abide in the prajnaparamita. There was no way out of this dilemma.

Then, inspired by Shariputra's questioning, Avalokiteshvara continued. He taught that when we understand that there is no final attainment, no ultimate answer or stopping place, when our mind is free of warring emotions and the belief in separateness, then we will have no fear. When I heard this many years ago, before I had any interest at all in a spiritual path, a little lightbulb went off: I definitely wanted to know more about "no fear."

This instruction on prajnaparamita is a teaching on fearlessness. To the extent that we stop struggling against uncertainty and ambiguity, to that extent we dissolve our fear. The synonym for total fearlessness is full enlightenment—wholehearted, open-minded inter-action with our world. Meanwhile we train in patiently moving in that direction. By learning to relax with groundlessness, we gradually connect with the mind that knows no fear.

Then Avalokiteshvara proclaimed the pith of the prajnaparamita, the essence of the rug-pulling-out experience, the essence of the fearless, open state of mind. It came in the form of a mantra: OM GATE GATE PARAGATE PARASAMGATE BODHI SVAHA. Just as a seed contains the tree, this mantra contains the entire teachings on abiding in prajnaparamita, abiding in the fearless state.

Trungpa Rinpoche's translation is "OM, gone, gone, gone beyond, gone completely beyond, awake, so be it." This is a description of a process, a journey, of always stepping out further and further. We could also say, "OM, groundlessness, groundlessness, more groundlessness, even beyond groundlessness, fully awake, so be it!"

No matter where we are on the bodhisattva path, whether we are just beginning or we've practiced for years, we're always stepping further into groundless-ness. Enlightenment is not the end of anything. Enlightenment, being completely awake, is just the beginning of fully entering into we know not what.

When the great bodhisattva finished teaching, the Buddha came out of his meditation and said, "Good, good! You expressed it perfectly, Avalokiteshvara." And those in the audience who hadn't walked out or died from heart attacks rejoiced. They rejoiced at hearing this teaching on stepping beyond fear.

19

Heightened Neurosis

> The "secret" of life that we are all looking for
> is just this: to develop through sitting and daily
> life practice the power and courage to return to
> that which we have spent a lifetime hiding from,
> to rest in the bodily experience of the present
> moment—even if it is a feeling of being humili-
> ated, of failing, of abandonment, of unfairness.
>
> —CHARLOTTE JŌKO BECK

WHEN WE TALK ABOUT RESTING in prajnaparamita, in unconditional bodhichitta, what
are we asking of ourselves? We are being encouraged to
remain open to the present groundless moment, to a
direct, unarmored participation with our experience.
We are certainly not being asked to trust that everything is going to be all right. Moving in the direction
of nothing to hold on to is daring. We will not initially experience it as a thrilling, alive, wonderful way to
be. How many of us feel ready to interrupt our habitual patterns, our almost instinctual ways of getting
comfortable?

We might assume that as we train in bodhichitta, our habitual patterns will start to unwind—that day by day, month by month, we'll be more open-minded, more flexible, more of a warrior. But what actually happens with ongoing practice is that our patterns intensify. In vajrayana Buddhism this is called "heightened neurosis." It's not something we do on purpose. It just happens. We catch the scent of groundlessness, and despite our wishes to remain steady, open, and flexible, we hold on tight in very habitual ways.

This has been the experience of everyone who ever set out on the path of awakening. All those smiling enlightened people you see in pictures or in person had to go through the process of encountering their full-blown neurosis, their methods of looking for ground. When we start to interrupt our ordinary ways of calling ourselves names and patting ourselves on the back, we are doing something extremely brave. Slowly we edge toward the open state, but let's face it, we are moving toward a place of no handholds, no footholds, no mindholds. This may be called liberation, but for a long time it feels like insecurity.

Let me give a few examples of heightened neuroses that actually develop *because* we practice. One is to develop a new self-critical story line based on spiritual ideals. We use the practice to reinforce poverty mentality: the warrior training becomes just one more way to feel that we never measure up. If we train to become a "good" warrior or to escape from being a "bad" person, then our thinking will remain just as polarized, just as stuck in right and wrong, as before. We will use the training against ourselves, trying to jump over issues that we're avoiding so as to attain some idealized notion of all-rightness. I'm not meaning to imply that this is unusual. Welcome to the human race. But because of our training we can start seeing clearly what we do and begin to practice compassionate inquiry into our own process. Psychologically what is happening to us? Do we feel inadequate? Do we continue to believe in our same old dramas?

There is also the opposite scenario. We use our training to feel superior, to increase our sense of being special. We are courageous to do this training. We are turning our lives around. We are proud to be doing something so rare in this world. We use the practice and teachings to build up our self-image and increase our arrogance and pride.

Another neurosis that can get heightened is avoidance. We wish to surrender our useless baggage, but in the process, we use the teachings themselves to distance ourselves from the chaotic, unsettling quality of our lives. In an attempt to avoid the fact that our partner is alcoholic or that we're addicted to marijuana or that we're in yet another abusive relationship, we earnestly train in relaxing into spaciousness, openness, warmheartedness. We try to use our spiritual training to avoid the queasy feeling in our gut.

The point is that we will bring our habitual ways of gluing ourselves together right into bodhichitta practice, right into the training in *un*gluing. If we want some insight into our habitual patterns, we can look at how we are relating to our practice, to the teachings and the teacher. Do we expect to have our needs met in the same way that we do in any neurotic relationship? Are we using spirituality to bypass what scares us? It's easy not to see that we are still seeking ground in the same old ways.

As we tentatively step out of our cocoon, we're bound to be afraid and grab on to what's familiar. Without ongoing patience and kindness toward this inevitable process, we will never trust that it's wise and compassionate to relax into the egoless state. We have to gradually develop the confidence that it is liberating to let go. Continually we train in maitri. It takes time to develop enthusiasm for how remaining open really feels.

A first step is to understand that a feeling of dread or psychological discomfort might just be a sign that old habits are getting liberated, that we are moving closer to the natural open state. Trungpa Rinpoche said that awakening warriors would find themselves in a constant state of anxiety. Personally, I've found this to be true. After a while I realized that since the shakiness wasn't going away, I might as well get to know it. When our attitude toward fear becomes more welcoming and inquisitive, there's a fundamental shift that occurs. Instead of spending our lives tensing up, as if we were in the dentist's chair, we learn that we can connect with the freshness of the moment and relax.

The practice is compassionate inquiry into our moods, our emotions, our thoughts. Practicing compassionate inquiry into our reactions and strategies is fundamental to the process of awakening. We are encouraged to be curious about the neurosis that's bound to kick in when our coping mechanisms start falling apart. This is how we get to the place where we stop believing in our personal myths, the place where we are not always divided against ourselves, always resisting our own energy. This is how we learn to abide in the prajnaparamita.

This is an ongoing practice. From the instant we begin this bodhisattva training until we completely trust the freedom of our unconditional, unbiased mind, we are surrendering moment by moment to whatever is happening in this very instant of time. With precision and gentleness, we surrender our cherished ways of regarding ourselves and others, our cherished ways of holding it all together, our cherished ways of blocking bodhichitta. We do this again and again over many challenging and inspiring years, and in the process develop an appetite for groundlessness.

20

When the Going Gets Rough

Don't be swayed by external circumstances.

—MIND-TRAINING SLOGAN OF ATISHA

THE MOST STRAIGHTFORWARD ADVICE ON awakening bodhichitta is this: practice not causing harm to anyone—yourself or others—and every day, do what you can to be helpful. If we take this instruction to heart and begin to use it, we will probably find that it is not so easy. Before we know it, someone has provoked us, and either directly or indirectly, we've caused harm.

Therefore, when our intention is sincere but the going gets rough, most of us could use some help. We could use some fundamental instruction on how to lighten up and turn around our well-established habits of striking out and blaming.

The four methods for holding our seat provide just such support for developing the patience to stay open to what's happening instead of acting on automatic pilot. These four methods are:

1. not setting up the target for the arrow,
2. connecting with the heart,
3. seeing obstacles as teachers, and
4. regarding all that occurs as a dream.

First, if we have not set up the target, it cannot be hit by an arrow. This is to say that each time we retaliate with aggressive words and actions, we are strengthening the habit of anger. As long as we do this, without doubt, plenty of arrows will come our way. We will become increasingly irritated by the reactions of others. However, each time we are provoked, we are given a chance to do something different. We can strengthen old habits by setting up the target or we can weaken them by holding our seat.

Each time we sit still with the restlessness and heat of anger, we are tamed and strengthened. This is instruction on cultivating the root of happiness. Each time we act on the anger or suppress it, we escalate our aggression; we become more and more like a walking target. Then, as the years go by, almost everything makes us mad. This is the key to understanding, at a completely real and personal level, how we sow the seeds of suffering.

So this is the first method: remember that we set up the target and only we can take it down. Understand that if we hold our seat when we want to retaliate— even if it's only briefly—we are starting to dissolve a pattern of aggression that will continue to hurt us and others forever if we let it.

Second is the instruction for connecting with the heart. In times of anger, we can contact the kindness and compassion that we already have.

When someone who is insane starts to harm us, we can easily understand that she doesn't know what she is doing. There is the possibility of contacting our heart and feeling sadness that she is out of control and is harming herself by hurting others. There is the possibility that even though we feel fear, we do not feel hatred or anger. Instead we might feel inspired to help this person if we can.

Actually, a lunatic is far less crazy than a sane person who harms us, for that so-called sane person has the potential to realize that in acting aggressively he is sowing seeds of his own confusion and dissatisfaction. His present aggression is strengthening future, more-intense habits of aggression. He is creating his own soap opera. This kind of life is painful and lonely. The one who harms us is under the influence of patterns that could continue to produce suffering forever.

So this is the second method: connect with the heart. Remember that the one who harms us does not need to be provoked further and neither do we. Recognize that, just like us, millions are burning with the fire of aggression. We can sit with the intensity of the anger and let its energy humble us and make us more compassionate.

Third is the instruction on seeing difficulties as teachers. If there is no teacher around to give us direct personal guidance on how to stop causing harm, never fear! Life itself will provide opportunities for learning how to hold our seat. Without the inconsiderate neighbor, where will we find the chance to practice patience? Without the office bully, how could we ever get the chance to know the energy of anger so intimately that it loses its destructive power?

The teacher is always with us. The teacher is always showing us precisely where we're at—encouraging us not to speak and act in the same old neurotic ways, encouraging us also not to repress or dissociate, encouraging us not to sow the seeds of suffering. So with this person who is scaring us or insulting us, do we retaliate as we have one hundred thousand times before, or do we start to get smart and finally hold our seat?

Right at the point when we are about to blow our top or withdraw into oblivion, we can remember this: we are warriors-in-training being taught how to sit with edginess and discomfort. We are being challenged to remain and to relax where we are.

The problem with following these or any instructions is that we have a tendency to be too serious and rigid. We get tense and uptight about trying to relax and be patient.

This is where the fourth instruction comes in: it is helpful to think about the person who is angry, the anger itself, and the object of that anger as being like a dream. We can regard our life as a movie in which we are temporarily the leading player. Rather than making it so important, we can reflect on the essencelessness of our current situation. We can slow down and ask ourselves, "Who is this monolithic me that has been so offended? And who is this other person who can trigger me like this? What is this praise and blame that hooks me like a fish, that catches me like a mouse in a trap? How is it that these circumstances have the power to propel me like a Ping-Pong ball from hope to fear, from happiness to misery?" This big-deal struggle, this big-deal self, and this big-deal other could all be lightened up considerably.

Contemplate these outer circumstances, as well as these emotions, as well as this huge sense of me, as passing and essenceless, like a memory, like a movie, like a dream. When we awaken from sleep we know that the enemies in our dreams are an illusion. That realization cuts through panic and fear.

When we find ourselves captured by aggression, we can remember this: there is no basis for striking out or for repressing. There is no basis for hatred or shame. We can at least begin to question our assumptions. Could it be that whether we are awake or asleep, we are simply moving from one dreamlike state to another?

These four methods for turning anger around and for learning a little patience come to us from the Kadampa masters of eleventh-century Tibet. These instructions have provided encouragement for fledgling bodhisattvas in the past, and they are just as useful in the present. These same Kadampa masters advised that we not procrastinate. They urged us to use these instructions immediately—on this very day in this very situation—and not say to ourselves, "I will try this in the future when I have a bit more time."

21

The Spiritual Friend

The real function of a spiritual friend is to
insult you.

—CHÖGYAM TRUNGPA RINPOCHE

WARRIORS-IN-TRAINING need someone to guide them—a master warrior, a teacher, a spiritual friend, someone who knows the territory well and can help them find their way. There are different levels of the teacher-student relationship. For some people, reading a book or hearing a specific teacher teach is enough. Others might then request to become that teacher's student—asking for guidance now and then. This kind of relationship is valuable for many. It is rare that students initially feel ready for a more unconditional commitment with a teacher, working very intimately on where they are holding back. Not many of us have that much trust in another person, that much willingness to be seen without our masks. We are wise, in fact, not to rush into such a relationship without developing maitri for ourselves and confidence that this particular teacher is trustworthy. These are the prerequisites for making a deeper commitment to a spiritual friend.

In 1974 when I asked Trungpa Rinpoche if I could be his student, I was not ready to enter into an unconditional relationship. But for the first time in my life I had met a person who was not caught up, a person whose mind was never swept away. I realized that with guidance from him, this was also possible for me. I was drawn to him because I couldn't manipulate him; he knew how to cut through people's trips. I experienced that cutting through as threatening, but in a very refreshing way. Still it took me years to develop enough trust and personal maitri to surrender to the relationship completely. Moving closer to someone who is so dangerous to the ego takes time.

Either the relationship with a teacher evolves to a place of unconditional trust and love, or it doesn't. We have to trust the process. In either case the relationship with a teacher encourages us to trust our basic wisdom. It teaches us to be steadfast with ourselves. In the warrior tradition it is said that both the teacher and the student are fully awake, that between the teacher and the student there can be a meeting of minds. The teacher's role is to help the student realize that his awakened mind and the teacher's are the same. At some point there's an important change of allegiance. Instead of always identifying with our neurosis, we begin to have confidence in our basic intelligence and kindness. This is a significant shift. Without developing this basic trust in ourselves, going further with a teacher is impossible.

Once we are ready to enter into an unconditional relationship, however, it teaches us how to be steadfast with every situation. Entering into this level of commitment to one person prepares us to stay open not only to the teacher but also to our whole experience. The teacher is a full-fledged human being, not some spiritual ideal. In this relationship, as in any other, we will experience likes and dislikes. We might find ourselves plunged right into the midst of chaos and insecurity. This relationship will show us if our heart is big enough to welcome the whole gamut of life—not just the part that we approve of. To the degree that we are capable of remaining steadfast with our spiritual friend, to this degree we can remain steadfast with the world as it is, with all its violence and tenderness, with its meanness and moments of courage. We find ourselves opening up in a way we never thought was possible.

Bodhisattva training encourages us to have a passionate involvement with life, regarding no emotion or action as unworthy of our love and compassion, regarding no person or situation as unacceptable. Therefore this path requires discipline and it also needs guidance. How much guidance we are ready to accept is the question. In the absence of a narrow, restrictive set of rules, we need someone to show us when we're off track, someone to whom we'll listen.

Whatever we do, the teacher is extraordinarily adaptable and loyal to the process of our awakening. This master warrior serves as a mirror that shows us our mind with embarrassing accuracy. The more we trust ourselves and the teacher, the more we allow this mirroring to happen. We slowly move in the direction of allowing every person we meet to be our teacher. We find ourselves more able to understand the mind-training slogan "Be grateful to everyone."

We don't, however, think of the teacher as having all the wisdom while we have none. There's too much hope and fear in that kind of setup. If I had been advised never to question my teachers, I wouldn't have lasted very long as a student. I was always encouraged to use my critical intelligence and express my concerns without fear. I was actually advised to question author-ity and rules.

It's important to understand that the minds of the teacher and the student meet, not by making the teacher all right or all wrong, but in the ambiguity between those two views, in the capacity to contain uncertainty and paradox. Otherwise our adulation inevitably flips into disillusionment. We bolt when the teacher doesn't fit our preconceptions. We don't like her political views or the fact that she eats meat, drinks alcohol, smokes cigarettes. We're out of there because we don't like a change in the organizational policy or because we feel unappreciated or neglected. We'll hang in for a honeymoon period, endowing the relationship with all our longings to be loved in an ideal, nonmessy way. Then inevitably our expectations are disappointed, and unresolved emotional issues arise. We feel used, betrayed, disillusioned. We don't want to feel these painful feelings and we leave.

The main point is always how we work with our minds. Once we click into solid views of justification or blaming, our minds become very small. Closing down in any form causes suffering to escalate. Our solid views could take the form of "the teacher is perfect and can do no wrong" or "the teacher is a charlatan and can never be trusted." Both are expressions of freezing the mind. We love to talk about vast, open mind, completely clear and spacious. But can we abide in the openness that presents itself when the bottom falls out of our dream?

Even if we do leave a teacher, if we can stay with the pain and disappointment without justifying or condemning, that teacher has taught us well. Practicing under such conditions may be the ultimate example of the slogan "If you can practice even when distracted, you are well trained."

In working with a spiritual friend we learn to love in an open-ended way—to love and to be loved unconditionally. We're not used to this kind of love. It's what we all want but what we all have difficulty giving. In my case I learned how to love and be loved by watching my teacher. When I saw how unconditionally he loved other people, I began to trust that he could also love me. I saw for myself what it means to never give up on anybody.

Something once happened along those lines that affected me profoundly. One of Trungpa Rinpoche's senior students, Joe, was having emotional difficulties, causing problems for everyone. Rinpoche seemed to ignore the other students' complaints about Joe's aggressive behavior. However, when Joe lashed out viciously at a woman and slapped her, Rinpoche yelled, "Out! I want you out of here now! I don't want to see your face again!" Joe left in shock. The other students gathered around Rinpoche, saying, "We're so glad you got rid of Joe. He did this terrible thing yesterday and that awful thing this morning. . . . Thank you for sending him away." Rinpoche drew himself up firmly and said: "I think you do not understand—Joe and I are the best of friends." I feel that Trungpa Rinpoche would have stepped in front of a speeding train if he thought it would help us wake up.

This unconditional commitment to ourselves and to others is what is meant by limitless love. The teacher's love for the student manifests as compassion. The student's love of the teacher is devotion. This mutual warmth, this heart connection, allows for a meeting of minds. It is this kind of love that tames untamable beings and helps bodhisattvas-in-training to go beyond their home ground. The relationship with our spiritual friend inspires us to step out fearlessly and start exploring the phenomenal world.

22

The In-Between State

The secret of Zen is just two words:
    not always so.

—SHUNRYU SUZUKI ROSHI

I t takes some training to equate complete letting go
with comfort. But in fact, "nothing to hold on to" is
the root of happiness. There's a sense of freedom when
we accept that we're not in control. Pointing ourselves
toward what we would most like to avoid makes our
barriers and shields permeable.

This may lead to a don't-know-what-to-do kind
of feeling, a sense of being caught in-between. On the
one hand, we're completely fed up with seeking comfort from what we can eat, drink, smoke, or couple
with. We're also fed up with beliefs, ideas, and "isms"
of all kinds. But on the other hand we wish it were true
that outer comfort could bring lasting happiness.

This in-between state is where the warrior spends
a lot of time growing up. We'd give anything to
have the comfort we used to get from eating a pizza or

watching a video. However, even though those things can be pleasurable, we've seen that eating a pizza or watching a video is a feeble match for our suffering. We notice this especially when things are falling apart. If we've just learned that we have cancer, eating a pizza doesn't do much to cheer us up. If someone we love has just died or walked out, the outer places we go for comfort feel feeble and ephemeral.

We are told about the pain of chasing after pleasure and the futility of running from pain. We hear also about the joy of awakening, of realizing our interconnectedness, of trusting the openness of our hearts and minds. But we aren't told all that much about this state of being in-between, no longer able to get our old comfort from the outside but not yet dwelling in a continual sense of equanimity and warmth.

Anxiety, heartbreak, and tenderness mark the in-between state. It's the kind of place we usually want to avoid. The challenge is to stay in the middle rather than buy into struggle and complaint. The challenge is to let it soften us rather than make us more rigid and afraid. Becoming intimate with the queasy feeling of being in the middle of nowhere only makes our hearts more tender. When we are brave enough to stay in the middle, compassion arises spontaneously. By not knowing, not hoping to know, and not acting like we know what's happening, we begin to access our inner strength.

Yet it seems reasonable to want some kind of relief.

If we can make the situation right or wrong, if we can pin it down in any way, then we are on familiar ground. But something has shaken up our habitual patterns and frequently they no longer work. Staying with volatile energy gradually becomes more comfortable than acting it out or repressing it. This open-ended tender place is called bodhichitta. Staying with it is what heals. It allows us to let go of our self-importance. It's how the warrior learns to love.

This is exactly how we're training every time we sit in meditation. We see what comes up, acknowledge that with kindness, and let go. Thoughts and emotions rise and fall. Some are more convincing than others. Habitually we are so uncomfortable with that churned-up feeling that we'd do anything to make it go away. Instead we kindly encourage ourselves to stay with our agitated energy by returning to the breath. This is the basic training in maitri that we need to just keep going forward, to just keep opening our heart.

Dwelling in the in-between state requires learning to contain the paradox of something's being both right and wrong, of someone's being strong and loving and also angry, uptight, and stingy. In that painful moment when we don't live up to our own standards, do we condemn ourselves or truly appreciate the paradox of being human? Can we forgive ourselves and stay in touch with our good and tender heart? When someone pushes our buttons, do we set out to make the person wrong? Or do we repress our reaction with

"I'm supposed to be loving. How could I hold this negative thought?" Our practice is to stay with the uneasiness and not solidify into a view. We can meditate, do tonglen, or simply look at the open sky— anything that encourages us to stay on the brink and not solidify into a view.

When we find ourselves in a place of discomfort and fear, when we're in a dispute, when the doctor says we need tests to see what's wrong, we'll find that we want to blame, to take sides, to stand our ground. We feel we must have some resolution. We want to hold our familiar view. For the warrior, "right" is as extreme a view as "wrong." They both block our innate wisdom. When we stand at the crossroads not knowing which way to go, we abide in prajnaparamita. The crossroads is an important place in the training of a warrior. It's where our solid views begin to dissolve.

Holding the paradox is not something any of us will suddenly be able to do. That's why we're encouraged to spend our whole lives training with uncertainty, ambiguity, insecurity. To stay in the middle prepares us to meet the unknown without fear; it prepares us to face both our life and our death. The in-between state—where moment by moment the warrior finds himself learning to let go—is the perfect training ground. It really doesn't matter if we feel depressed about that or inspired. There is absolutely no way to do this just right. That's why compassion and maitri, along with courage, are vital: they give us the resources to be genuine about where we are, but at the same time to know that we are always in transition, that the only time is now, and that the future is completely unpredictable and open.

As we continue to train, we evolve beyond the little me who continually seeks zones of comfort. We gradually discover that we are big enough to hold something that is neither lie nor truth, neither pure nor impure, neither bad nor good. But first we have to appreciate the richness of the groundless state and hang in there.

It's important to hear about this in-between state. Otherwise we think the warrior's journey is one way or the other; either we're all caught up or we're free. The fact is that we spend a long time in the middle. This juicy spot is a fruitful place to be. Resting here completely—steadfastly experiencing the clarity of the present moment—is called enlightenment.

Concluding Aspiration

Throughout my life, until this very moment, whatever
virtue I have accomplished, including any benefit that
may come from this book, I dedicate to the welfare of
all beings.

May the roots of suffering diminish. May warfare,
violence, neglect, indifference, and addictions
also decrease.

May the wisdom and compassion of all beings increase,
now and in the future.

May we clearly see all the barriers we erect between ourselves and others to be as insubstantial as our
dreams.

May we appreciate the great perfection of all
phenomena.

May we continue to open our hearts and minds,
in order to work ceaselessly for the benefit of
all beings.

May we go to the places that scare us.

May we lead the life of a warrior.

APPENDIX: PRACTICES

The Mind-Training Slogans of Atisha

POINT ONE
*The Preliminaries, Which Are a Basis
for Dharma Practice*

    1. First, train in the preliminaries.

POINT TWO
*The Main Practice, Which Is Training
in Bodhichitta*

ULTIMATE BODHICHITTA SLOGANS

    2. Regard all dharmas as dreams.

    3. Examine the nature of unborn awareness.

    4. Self-liberate even the antidote.

    5. Rest in the nature of alaya, the essence.

    6. In postmeditation, be a child of illusion.

RELATIVE BODHICHITTA SLOGANS

    7. Sending and taking should be practiced
       alternately.
       These two should ride the breath.

    8. Three objects, three poisons, and three seeds
       of virtue.

9. In all activities, train with slogans.
10. Begin the sequence of sending and taking with yourself.

POINT THREE
*Transformation of Bad Circumstances
into the Path of Enlightenment*

11. When the world is filled with evil,
    Transform all mishaps into the path of bodhi.
12. Drive all blames into one.
13. Be grateful to everyone.
14. Seeing confusion as the four kayas
    Is unsurpassable shunyata protection.
15. Four practices are the best of methods.
16. Whatever you meet unexpectedly, join with meditation.

POINT FOUR
*Showing the Utilization of Practice
in One's Whole Life*

17. Practice the five strengths,
    The condensed heart instructions.
18. The mahayana instruction for ejection
    of consciousness at death
    Is the five strengths: how you conduct yourself
    is important.

POINT FIVE
Evaluation of Mind Training

19. All dharma agrees at one point.

20. Of the two witnesses, hold the principal one.
21. Always maintain only a joyful mind.
22. If you can practice even when distracted, you are well trained.

POINT SIX
Disciplines of Mind Training

23. Always abide by the three basic principles.
24. Change your attitude, but remain natural.
25. Don't talk about injured limbs.
26. Don't ponder others.
27. Work with the greatest defilements first.
28. Abandon any hope of fruition.
29. Abandon poisonous food.
30. Don't be so predictable.
31. Don't malign others.
32. Don't wait in ambush.
33. Don't bring things to a painful point.
34. Don't transfer the ox's load to the cow.
35. Don't try to be the fastest.
36. Don't act with a twist.
37. Don't make gods into demons.
38. Don't seek others' pain as the limbs of your own happiness.

POINT SEVEN
Guidelines of Mind Training

39. All activities should be done with one intention.
40. Correct all wrongs with one intention.

41. Two activities: one at the beginning, one at the end.
42. Whichever of the two occurs, be patient.
43. Observe these two, even at the risk of your life.
44. Train in the three difficulties.
45. Take on the three principal causes.
46. Pay heed that the three never wane.
47. Keep the three inseparable.
48. Train without bias in all areas.
    It is crucial always to do this pervasively and wholeheartedly.
49. Always meditate on whatever provokes resentment.
50. Don't be swayed by external circumstances.
51. This time, practice the main points.
52. Don't misinterpret.
53. Don't vacillate.
54. Train wholeheartedly.
55. Liberate yourself by examining and analyzing.
56. Don't wallow in self-pity.
57. Don't be jealous.
58. Don't be frivolous.
59. Don't expect applause.

The Four Limitless Ones Chant

May all sentient beings enjoy happiness and the root
   of happiness.
May they be free from suffering and the root of suffering.
May they not be separated from the great happiness
   devoid of suffering.
May they dwell in the great equanimity free from passion,
   aggression, and prejudice.

Each line of this chant refers to one of the four limitless
qualities: the first, loving-kindness; the second, compassion; the third, rejoicing; and the fourth, equanimity. I
sometimes prefer to change the word *they* to *we*. This
change emphasizes that we aspire to experience the benefit
of these four qualities ourselves, along with other beings.

Loving-Kindness Practice

The practice of loving-kindness traditionally uses the first line of the Four Limitless Ones chant, "May all sentient beings enjoy happiness and the root of happiness."

1. Awaken loving-kindness for yourself. "May I enjoy happiness and the root of happiness," or put this aspiration in your own words.
2. Awaken loving-kindness for someone for whom you feel sincere goodwill and tenderness. "May (name) enjoy happiness and the root of happiness," or choose your own words.
3. Awaken loving-kindness for a friend, again saying the friend's name and expressing the aspiration for his or her happiness, using the same words.
4. Awaken loving-kindness for someone about whom you feel neutral or indifferent. (Use the same words.)
5. Awaken loving-kindness for someone you find difficult or offensive. (Use the same words.)
6. Let the loving-kindness grow big enough to include all the beings in the five steps above. (This step is called "dissolving the barriers.") Say, "May I, my beloved, my friend, the neutral person, the difficult person, all together enjoy happiness and the root of happiness."
7. Extend loving-kindness toward all beings throughout the universe. You can start close to home and widen the circle more and more. "May all beings enjoy happiness and the root of happiness."

Compassion Practice

The compassion practice begins with the second line of the chant, "May we be free from suffering and the root of suffering," and then follows a seven-step process similar to that of the loving-kindness practice.

1. Awaken compassion toward yourself: "May I be free from suffering and the root of suffering," or put this aspiration in your own words.
2. Awaken compassion for a person (or animal) for whom you already feel spontaneous compassion: "May (name) be free from suffering and the root of suffering," or choose your own words.
3. Awaken compassion for a friend. (Use the same words.)
4. Awaken compassion for someone about whom you feel neutral. (Use the same words.)
5. Awaken compassion for someone you find difficult. (Use the same words.)
6. Awaken compassion for all five of the beings above. (Use the same words.)
7. Awaken compassion for all beings throughout the universe, starting close to home and extending out further and further: "May all beings be free of suffering and the root of suffering."

You may also awaken the ability to rejoice and the capacity for equanimity by going through the seven steps as before. You can use your own words or you can use the third line of the Four Limitless Ones chant for rejoicing ("May I and all others never be separated from the great happiness devoid of suffering"). You can use the fourth line of the chant for equanimity ("May I and others dwell in the great equanimity free from passion, aggression, and prejudice").

The Three-Step Aspiration

May I enjoy happiness and the root of happiness.
May you enjoy happiness and the root of happiness.
May all beings enjoy happiness and the root of
    happiness.

You can use this same three-step process to awaken
compassion, the ability to rejoice, and equanimity. As
always, it is fine to use your own words.

BIBLIOGRAPHY

GENERAL TEACHINGS ON BODHICHITTA

Patrul Rinpoche. *The Words of My Perfect Teacher*. Translated by the Padmakara Translation Group. Boston and London: Shambhala Publications, 1998, pp. 195–261.

Shantideva. *The Way of the Bodhisattva*. Translated by the Padmakara Translation Group. Boston and London: Shambhala Publications, 1997.

———. *A Guide to the Bodhisattva's Way of Life*. Translated by Stephen Batchelor. Dharamsala: Library of Tibetan Works and Archives, 1998.

Sogyal Rinpoche. *The Tibetan Book of Living and Dying*. Edited by Patrick Gaffney and Andrew Harvey. San Francisco: HarperSanFrancisco, 1993.

Trungpa, Chögyam. *Cutting Through Spiritual Materialism*. Boston and London: Shambhala Publications, 1987, pp. 167–216.

———. *The Myth of Freedom*. Boston and London: Shambhala Publications, 1988, pp. 103–26.

THE FOUR LIMITLESS QUALITIES

Kamalashila. *Meditation: The Buddhist Way of Tranquility and Insight*. Glasgow: Windhorse, 1992, pp. 23–32, 192–206.

Longchenpa. *Kindly Bent to Ease Us.* Translated by H. V. Guenther. Berkeley: Dharma Publications, 1975–76, pp. 106–22.

Patrul Rinpoche. *The Words of My Perfect Teacher.* Translated by the Padmakara Translation Group. Boston and London: Shambhala Publications, 1998, pp. 195–217.

Salzberg, Sharon. *Lovingkindness: The Revolutionary Art of Happiness.* Boston and London: Shambhala Publications, 1995.

Thich Nhat Hanh. *Teachings on Love.* Berkeley: Parallax Press, 1997.

THE LOJONG SLOGANS

Chödrön, Pema. *Start Where You Are: A Guide to Compassionate Living.* Boston and London: Shambhala Publications, 1994.

Khyentse, Dilgo. *Enlightened Courage.* Ithaca, N.Y.: Snow Lion Publications, 1993.

Kongtrul, Jamgon. *The Great Path of Awakening: A Commentary on the Mahayana Teaching of the Seven Points of Mind Training.* Boston and London: Shambhala Publications, 1987.

Trungpa, Chögyam. *Training the Mind and Cultivating Loving-Kindness.* Edited by Judith L. Lief. Boston and London: Shambhala Publications, 1993.

Wallace, Alan B. *A Passage from Solitude: Training the Mind in a Life Embracing the World.* Edited by Zara Houshmand. Ithaca, N.Y.: Snow Lion Publications, 1992.

TONGLEN PRACTICE

Chödrön, Pema. *Tonglen: The Path of Transformation.*
Edited by Tingdzin Ötro. Halifax, N.S.: Vajradhatu
Publications, 2001.

Sogyal Rinpoche. *The Tibetan Book of Living and Dying.*
Edited by Patrick Gaffney and Andrew Harvey. San
Francisco: HarperSanFrancisco, 1993, pp. 201–8.

ADDITIONAL READING

Masters, Jarvis Jay. *Finding Freedom: Writings from Death
Row.* Junction City, Calif.: Padma Publishing, 1997.

Suzuki, Shunryu. *Zen Mind, Beginner's Mind.* Boston and
London: Shambhala Publications, 1996.

Trungpa, Chögyam. *Shambhala: The Sacred Path of the
Warrior.* Boston and London: Shambhala Publications,
1984.

RESOURCES

For information regarding meditation instruction
or inquiries about a practice center near you, please
contact one of the following:

Shambhala International
1084 Tower Road
Halifax, Nova Scotia
Canada B3H 2Y5
phone: (902) 425-4275
fax: (902) 423-2750
website: www.shambhala.org

Shambhala Europe
Annostrasse 27-33
D50678 Köln, Germany
phone: 49-221-31024-10
fax: 49-221-31024-50
e-mail: europe@shambhala.org

Karmê Chöling
369 Patneaude Lane
Barnet, VT 05821
phone: (802) 633-2384
fax: (802) 633-3012
e-mail: karmecholing@shambhala.org

Shambhala Mountain Center
4921 County Road 68C
Red Feather Lakes, CO 80545
phone: (970) 881-2184
fax: (970) 881-2909
e-mail: rmsc@shambhala.org

Gampo Abbey
Pleasant Bay, Nova Scotia
Canada BOE 2P0
phone: (902) 224-2752
e-mail: office@gampoabbey.org

Naropa University is the only accredited, Buddhist-
inspired university in North America. For more
information, contact:

Naropa University
2130 Arapahoe Avenue
Boulder, CO 80302
phone: (303) 444-0202
website: www.naropa.edu

Audio- and videotape recordings of talks
and seminars by Pema Chödrön are available from:

Great Path Tapes and Books
330 East Van Hoesen Boulevard
Portage, MI 49002
phone: (269) 384-4167
fax: (425) 940-8456

e-mail: gptapes@aol.com
website: www.pemachodrontapes.org

Kalapa Recordings
1084 Tower Road
Halifax, Nova Scotia
Canada B3J 2Y5
phone: (902) 420-1118, ext. 19
fax: (902) 423-2750
e-mail: shop@shambhala.org
website: www.shambhalashop.com

Sounds True
735 Walnut Street
Boulder, CO 80302
phone: (800) 333-9185
website: www.soundstrue.com

BOOKS AND AUDIO
BY PEMA CHÖDRÖN

BOOKS

Always Maintain a Joyful Mind: And Other Lojong Teachings on Awakening Compassion and Fearlessness

In this book Pema Chödrön introduces fifty-nine pith teachings (called *lojong* in Tibetan) and offers guidance on how to make them part of our everyday lives. The book also features a forty-five-minute audio program entitled "Opening the Heart," in which Pema Chödrön offers in-depth instruction on *tonglen* meditation, a powerful practice that anyone can undertake to awaken compassion for oneself and others.

Awakening Loving-Kindness

Selected readings from *The Wisdom of No Escape*, presented in a small pocket-sized edition, perfect for carrying along in a purse, briefcase, or coat pocket. A portable book of inspiration on how to remain wholeheartedly awake and use the abundant material of daily life as your primary teacher and guide.

Comfortable with Uncertainty: 108 Teachings on Cultivating Fearlessness and Compassion

This book offers short, stand-alone readings designed to help us cultivate compassion and awareness amid the challenges of daily living. More than a collection of thoughts for the day, *Comfortable with Uncertainty* offers a progressive program of spiritual study, leading the reader through essential concepts, themes, and practices on the Buddhist path.

No Time to Lose: A Timely Guide to the Way of the Bodhisattva

In this book Pema Chödrön presents the traditional Buddhist teachings that guide her own life: those of The *Way of the Bodhisattva (Bodhicharyavatara)*, a text written by the eighth-century sage Shantideva. This treasured Buddhist work is remarkably relevant for our times, describing the steps we can take to cultivate courage, caring, and joy—the keys to healing ourselves and our troubled world.

The Places That Scare You: A Guide to Fearlessness in Difficult Times

We always have a choice, Pema Chödrön teaches: We can let the circumstances of our lives harden us and make us increasingly resentful and afraid, or we can let them soften us and make us kinder. Amid our difficulties, wisdom is always available to us, but we usually block it with habitual patterns rooted in fear. Beyond that fear lies a state of open-heartedness and tenderness. This book teaches us how to awaken our basic goodness and connect with others, to accept ourselves and others complete with faults and imperfections.

Practicing Peace in Times of War

"War and peace begin in the hearts of individuals," declares Pema Chödrön. She explains that, remarkably, the way in which we as individuals respond to challenges in our everyday lives can mean the difference between perpetuating a culture of violence or creating a new culture of compassion. In this book Pema Chödrön insists that our world will begin to change when each of us, one by one, begins to work for peace at the level of our own behavior, our own habits of thought and action. It's never too late, she tells us, to look within and discover a new way of living.

Start Where You Are: A Guide to Compassionate Living

An indispensable handbook for cultivating fearlessness and awakening compassion in the midst of daily living. Pema Chödrön frames her teachings on compassion around fifty-nine traditional Tibetan Buddhist maxims such as: "Always apply only a joyful state of mind" and "Always meditate on whatever provokes resentment."

When Things Fall Apart: Heart Advice for Difficult Times

Drawing on traditional Buddhist wisdom, here is radical

and compassionate advice for what to do when our lives become painful and difficult. There is only one approach to suffering that is of lasting benefit, Pema teaches, and that approach involves moving toward painful situations with friendliness and curiosity. This book includes instructions on how to use painful emotions to cultivate wisdom, compassion, and courage; how to communicate in a way that leads to openness and true intimacy with others; and how to reverse negative habitual patterns.

The Wisdom of No Escape: And the Path of Loving-Kindness

A book about saying yes to life in all its manifestations, embracing the potent mixture of joy, suffering, brilliance, and confusion that characterizes the human experience. Pema Chödrön shows us the profound value of our situation of "no escape" from the ups and downs of life.

AUDIO

Don't Bite the Hook: Finding Freedom from Anger, Resentment, and Other Destructive Emotions

In this recorded weekend retreat, Pema draws on Buddhist teachings to show us how to relate constructively to the inevitable shocks, losses, and frustrations of life so that we can find true happiness. The key, Pema explains, is not biting the "hook" of our habitual responses.

Practicing Peace in Times of War: Four Talks

The book *Practicing Peace in Times of War* is based on several of Pema Chödrön's public talks, and we are proud to present them to you here, in this audio edition. It is a short, pithy, and profound work that includes practical strategies for cultivating the seeds of peace and compassion amid life's upsets and challenges.

This Moment Is the Perfect Teacher

Lojong is a powerful Tibetan Buddhist practice created especially for training the mind to work with the challenges of everyday living. It teaches our hearts to soften, reframes our attitude toward difficulty, and allows us to discover a wellspring of inner strength. In this recorded retreat, Pema Chödrön introduces the lojong teachings and explains how we can apply them to any situation in our life—because, as Pema says, "every moment is an opportunity for awakening."

When Things Fall Apart

This abridged audiobook based on the beloved spiritual classic contains radical and compassionate advice for what to do when our lives become painful and difficult. Read by Pema, it includes instructions on how to use painful emotions to cultivate wisdom, compassion, and courage; how to communicate in a way that leads to openness and true intimacy with others; and how to reverse negative habitual patterns.